THE SUPPER CLUB

Justin Thadd Kludzinski

Edited by: Marie Lottie Kludzinski

authorHOUSE®

AuthorHouse™
1663 Liberty Drive
Bloomington, IN 47403
www.authorhouse.com
Phone: 1-800-839-8640

Published by AuthorHouse 04/23/2014

ISBN: 978-1-4969-0605-2 (sc)
ISBN: 978-1-4969-0606-9 (e)

Library of Congress Control Number: 2014907232

Contents

Maria

Dedication

I would like to dedicate my second book to the loving memory of my late wife Maria. Maria and I were married for 32 years when she died of cancer in the ides of March 2013. We have two great children a daughter and a son. I had known her for many years. She was my sister's best friend growing up. I remember them playing the Osmond's record "One Bad Apple" over and over again when I got home from work. I was such a grouch. I would tell them to stop playing it. I then went in the Army. Maria went to school in Honduras for a year during my last year in the Army. I had grown up to be a better man. Maria had learned her customs and really learns to dance. I had done the same while in the Army ranks. She was a beautiful woman. She was not that teen bop girl I had left three years before. I was going to the discos every weekend with my brother as my wingman. We had hit them all. I found out from my sister that Maria liked to dance so I asked her out on a date and it led to our romance. I still remember the first song that we danced to in my basement before we went out. It was the Four Seasons "Oh What a Night" so that became our song. We had a lot of love and planned our every move. The talks at night were great right after we made love. I miss those most of all. My left side of the bed is empty without her stealing heat as we did like to spoon. I miss the smell of the perfume she wore her Cachet, Hawaiian White Ginger, and Jean Nate. I do not hear her voice. Her cat pixie is sad. I cannot see her pretty face, but I hope she is still around. I wake up at dawn, and look just to my left, and she is nowhere to be found. I wonder if love does die or is it transcended to God's heaven above. I know Maria will be in my heart. The bell does toll for all people. That is the way it must be done. I hope that the future is brighter, but it is bittersweet without you. A kiss of love is all that I can bring.

The Main Characters

Katy Scherry: She is a very outspoken girl and might curse without thinking. She is originally from Cleveland, OH and is of Greek ancestry. She has jet black hair and a wicked smile. She talks about romance like I have never heard any girl talk about before. She may act tough, but deep down there is a Jane Austen soft side to her. She is a talker and doctors have snuck out on her, because time is of no concern to her. We once went to a baseball game and when we picked up Katy, we turned the radio off. We could not hear the music, so we just listened to her stories. I remember when we all were such close friends. It saddens me to know it can never be the same.

Greg Krasinski: He is a really good guy and very generous. Greg thinks about others before himself. He has a good sense of humor. As patrol boys we used to guard the same crossing on 83rd street and Brandon Avenue located in the Bush area of Chicago. One day Greg and I gave the 6th graders penance to write 100 times no crossing the street until we gave the okay. We did not have that kind of authority, but we figured if it works, why fight it. I have known Greg for many years. I went to school with him since the 2nd grade through high school. He loves sports and was our catcher on our White Sox little league team. We collected Mars invader cards, built planes, and played Combat.

Young Lee: I know Korea is a land far away, but you taught me things to say in Korean. You said lets go dancing is "ui chum-eul gaja." You also taught me how to say white wine, "baegpodoju." You also taught me lobster "saeu." You taught me a cleaner way to eat lunch. You always opened a napkin, and then put down your food on the napkin to avoid germs. I still do it today. I remember you with kindness, and the book you gave me on Korean culture. I used to fix your machine first when others did not see, because you were a special girl I had come to know. She had very pretty black hair, a smile that made you feel good inside, eyes that saw your soul, and a heart of love to show the world.

Steve Key: He was the youngest of his family. He had an older brother and two older sisters who were always saying, "Boy is Steve good looking." I think this was good, but part of me thinks it was bad, only because it put pressure on him to always be with the best looking girl. I know he has a kind heart; he loves his family very much. He always talks a big game, but I have seen how much he cares. There is no better friend. He is a party dude; he always wants to have fun. He bowled with us on the Hunks, our bowling team. He is a Cubs fan like me and goes to many games. He hops on the old red line "L" to Addison Street. I still remember when my dad took Steve, Stan, and I to Channel Lake to go fishing in his white top and black Biscayne Chevy. A cop stopped us for supposedly blowing a stop sign and my dad slipped him a five dollar bill the old Chicago way.

Tara Nelson: She is a very friendly girl once she gets to know you, and she always speaks her mind. She really likes pizza. We sometimes ate pizza in the evenings at work. Working as a nurse to sick people is her calling. She talks them through the rough stuff. We went to a baseball game once with most of my family. It was her first White Sox game, and she had a lot of fun. We went to Dunkin Donuts to get our free coffee we won at the game. We wanted doughnuts too, but the guy at Dunkin Donuts told us he was out of doughnuts. It was funny because we could see a big tray of doughnuts behind him. Her foot needed some surgery, so she was off from work for a time. I told her that I would help her set up a router for her laptop. Her son was playing football with his little cousin. I told them to take turns covering for each other while I threw the ball. Tara sat on the porch watching as the kids and I played football for awhile.

Ken Kowalkowski: This is one smart guy. He always studied hard. I met Ken when I was in 4th grade and Ken was in 2nd grade. We were all playing a tackle football game in the cigar box part of Russell Square Park. Greg lived across the alley from Ken and invited him to join us. Ken was a straight ahead runner and hard to tackle like fullbacks of old. We have been friends ever since. Ken and I still go fishing at Lemon Lake. He cares about everyone in the group and visits us when we are sick. He went on to be a CPA, but his good heart never gets in his way. I think my cousin Wanda used to call him a holy roller because he did not curse. I now see that to fall to peer pressure is to lose yourself and Ken never did.

Greg Krasinski

Act 1

Chaos at ORD

"What baggage claim terminal are we going to Tara?" "We are going to United #3, Young." We don't have to hurry as I look at the board because they are 15 minutes late. "I can't wait to see Katy and her little sister Melanie. She has never been anywhere else but Cleveland. We have to hit some Disco dance clubs. I hope we can get her in. Young are you talking about Melanie or Katy?" They both laugh. "I am taller and I am Korean. I am supposed to be short. I sure do miss her. She is the best talker of the group. We have not been out on a date or met any guys since she left. We better not tell her that, or she will just give us the business. Tara there she is! There is her little bigger sister Melanie." "Young she must have put on some weight. Home cooking agrees with her. Right now she is three digits big deal. Hey! Flock my little sister Melanie." "Hi! I am Young and tall." "Hi! I am Tara and cooler. What the heck have you been up to?" "Nothing, I wasn't' here to find guys for you. Don't let my big sister boss you around like that. She does that the best." "Watch it sis or I'll send you on next plane back to Cleveland. Let's get our luggage and get going." "Yes! Mother Goose we are going. Which ones are ours?" Just then Steve and Ken get to the same baggage terminal. Greg is getting back for his 3 year hitch with the U.S. Army. He was a medic and been to Nam, but after the war he was stationed in Germany. He was in Munich with a tank unit, the 3rd Army 63rd division. His draft number was up at 41, so he joins to be a medic. He took his AIT at Fort Sam Houston in Texas. His friend Ken is a graduated and licensed CPA. He is taking an old friend out on the town to some disco to meet some new girls. Then there's Steve, the constant student playboy of the group. He is the one with all the lines and good looks and Dad's money to make it a great night out for the return of

1

their friend, the war hero. Just then Katy says," Tara there they are! Those are our blue American Touristor luggages, get them!" Tara leans over to get them, and gets a very well devised glance by Steve. Katy notices as she is good at spotting bad body language. She says to Steve, "You always check out girls' butts." He being a total wise guy says, "Only those that are booty lushes." Greg just gets there in his Army Khakis all decked out. Katy says to him, "Put your friend back in a cage and focus your eyes on something else." Greg says, "What about your pretty face?" "These brown eyes are not going there." Some random hippie said, "Yeah baby killers" to Greg. Tara said, "Shut your mouth punk. What have you ever done for your country?" Katy shouted at him, "My brown eyes would rather look at him then at scum like you." The hippie left and just walked away. Steve said, "Yeah go on leave, that's what you guys are good at doing going to Canada." Greg said, "Thanks it has been that way for my 3 years when I have been stateside." "Greg do not let it bug you; we know what you guys did for us." "Hi! I am Ken. These are my friends, Greg the army dude and Steve the guy with good eye sight." "Hi! I am Katy." "This is my little sis Melanie, and my flock Young and Tara," the object of Steve's eyes. They all exchange greetings and say, "Maybe we will see each other at some disco clubs later." "We'll see you later I hope," as the guys leave with fake phone numbers. The girls just laugh. Young said, "I got a feeling we will see them again." Katy said, "I do too." Melanie said, "Let's load up the old green 1969 Impala. Let's get out of dodge. I can't wait till we get back to our beautiful Victorian house." "Hey! Brat you shouldn't make fun of Dad's old car. It gets us girls all over town with room in the trunk for your junk." Tara says, "I like this heap and so does Young. There is a lot of room at the drive-in if you know what I mean."

Katy says, "You and Young have been going to the drive-in with those high school hippies again drinking that Boon's Farm Apple. What a bunch of runners. You guys did not get any hickeys when I was gone? I am checking your necks, and I better not see a scarf around them."

Young says, "Yes number one mom, we were good." They both laugh. "Melanie jump in! What do you think about that army dude Greg?" "He looked pretty good to me." Katy said, "He was alright, but he seen the world. He does not need to hang out with jail bait from high school like you." Young says," I think Katy might want him for herself." "He's not my speed," Katy says. Tara says, "He is your speed Katy, remember Dennis?" "I do, but he was Navy and I was dumb so let us drop it." Katy says, "I guess I will always be a happily ever after romantic." "Wait a minute this blue/green eyed little sister is not just giving him to you." "He is not even hers yet," Tara says. "I know Katy," Young says, "That will not stop her." They all laugh, park the car in front of the house they rented on Belmont and Clark Street, and unloaded the car, suitcases and called it a night. The guys got Greg's stuff and packed it in Steve's 1968 Buick Electra, with Greg getting shotgun even though Ken called it. "I guess I'll give it to you since you went to Nam, and were a hero and stuff." Greg says, "Thanks most honorable sir." Steve says, "Yeah he has been telling all the girls we knew at the club you have been in jail for the last 3 years. But don't get mad Ken I'm just pulling your leg." Ken says, "Steve you are always so full of it." Steve said, "I get the ladies that way right Greg?" "It did help us with that great Greek chick and her fine soul sister friend. And also with her Miss high IQ Korean friend and the good looking but lock me up now high school kid. Steve yeah bro, I really dug that soul sister. What a brick house!" Ken chimed in, "The Korean was the only one that talked English that made sense. Her name was Young. She sure looked good and was very smart." "I guess married joint with 6 figures is what matters to you Ken," said Steve. Greg says, "It sounds corny but I am looking for real romance, like fireworks, like love American style stuff." "That's crazy talk says Steve, you've been in the jungle too long." Ken says, "You do not know enough about her. She might be a real space cadet and not to smart." Greg says, "Well dudes this is Steve's place, Lake Point Towers. I'm glad his dad is rich. Let's dump his stuff in my apartment and get to Mother's. I have a seven/seven with my name on it, and some hot chick to find me. I need a drink after that. It better be some tequila instead, I need a lot of it. Ken, I guess I must be the wing man again. Let's get going. My family thinks that I get back tomorrow. I really need a night out first, before I get the cookies and what are you going do now speech from my Mom." "You've got to let go and party," said Steve as we left.

Young Lee

Act 2

Selectric

It was the last day of registration and school started that night. Downtown Northwestern University is a cool looking school right by Lake Michigan. Steve and Ken had asked me why I was taking this journalism course 201. I told Steve it was to pick up chicks. I told Ken it would help me in my technical writing. The truth is I was taking it for myself to grow and write anything I learned in life, and have fun with it. "Hi! Steve, Greg and Ken," said Tara when we met last week at the airport. "I was wondering if someone so beautiful like you would remember a good looking guy like me," said Steve to Tara. "Hi! Ken, Greg and Steve," said Young as she came out of the bathroom to join Tara. She said, "What are you boys up too?" Ken says, "Journalism 201 class is tonight." "That's great, that's what all three of us are taking," said Young. "I only see two of you," Greg says to Young. "I was wondering if you noticed Katy wasn't here," Tara replied. "Young doesn't worry, Greg she is at the book store. That's our girl little miss Girl Scout, who wants to have all the books the first day." "Tara, you're too hard on her she just likes to plan ahead. I think that she's right. See you guys in class," says Greg as he heads for the book store. "Tara, how about you and Young joining me and Ken for some cafeteria coffee, I'm buying. Let's blow this bursar's office. Steve your dad's loaded, can you spring for some donuts? Also, I am a little light after the bursar cleaned me out." "Sure, whatever you and my foxes want," said Steve." "I beg your pardon Steve, this little fox is into Ken not you" said Young. "That's a first for me," says Ken. "What Steve wants with the ladies, Steve gets." Tara says, "We will see what Steve gets." The girls both laugh. They all head to the same class they were in, Journalism 201. Katy and Greg were already talking to each other like old friends of 10 years. Tara says to

Young, "Check out Katy she is moving in on Greg." Young says, "Look! She is twirling her hair. That's her sign for us to back off." "Hey! Steve, come sit over here at my desk with me," says Tara. "Sure pretty lady I knew you would come around," said Steve. "Ken I don't want to sit alone or with some frat girl," said Young. There were all girls in the class except for us three, Ken noticed. We soon had seen why. Gail Storm, who is from CBS channel 2 news, is our teacher. She told the aide to put a Selectric typewriter, 2 on each desk table. Greg said to Katy, "It looks like my old high school physics lab minus the Bunsen burner of course." Katy said, "I love these typewriters they are so modern." Gail starts the class by saying, "For your first assignment type a thousand word story now about the rise and fall of the Roman Empire." The girls all spring into action typing their little fingers off. Steve looked at me. I looked at Ken, who then looked at Steve. We all said it together, "She hates guys and wants us out of the class." The class ends in disaster. We guys never felt so low, completely bombing our first assignment. Katy seen we were down. She said, "Hey guys don't let the old witch win. Tara, Young and I are great typists, we can teach you." Ken said, "I think we should drop the class." Steve said, "She hates us bad." Greg said, "I am not quitting because of her. Shakespeare never knew how to type and he was a great writer. Let's see what Katy, Tara and Young can teach us." "I'll give it a try if I get to see Tara in her P.J's with all that night typing we will be doing. Hey! Ken, remember to take your shoes off in Young's room. She looks good in her oriental PJ's," said Steve. Katy said, "It will be in the library, not in our rooms." Tara said, "Katy you talk too much sometimes." Then all the girls laugh.

Greg said, "I don't care if it's at the library or your house Katy. I think we should buy you girls a late dinner or supper for helping us out each time."

Ken says, "I got it like a supper club that meets like at a smoker." Young says, "You got it Ken. We will call our group the supper club." "I like it," Greg says. Katy says, "I like it too. Make sure that for me, it has to have a great salad selection." "Yes Mom," said Tara and Young tighter with a laugh. Steve said, "It's going to be on me." Ken said, "Your dad can afford it." They continue talking about it until they get to their cars. Then Tara and Young had twisted Katy's arm that they were to meet the next night at their house. They would go to supper first, and then hit the typewriters until at least 12:00AM. Longer for Steve was better. I do think Tara was too smart to let Steve get out of control so fast. The restaurant was an Italian place called Club El Bianco's. They exchanged phone numbers. Then they said their goodbyes, and hugs went all around. The Greg and Katy one lasted the longest. Ken noticed was our boy Greg falling into Katy's brown eyed pool of romance?

Melanie Scherry

Act 3

Cena

Greg, Ken, and Steve were the first to get to the restaurant on 63rd street and Troy Avenue. They had been there many times with the old gang. We always order the 12 course Italian meal, and pick someone for whose birthday is it this time trick. It was Young's turn this time because she took the longest in the bathroom. First we had a great salad with hot bread and olive oil, followed by a small dish of Ravioli. Next our wine arrives, along with a cheese plate and crackers. Then our main entrees arrive which consist of lasagna, eggplant parmesan, spaghetti and meatballs, Chicken Alfredo, veal parmesan, and linguine. For dessert we have fresh fruit, Italian ice, and Tiramisu. I think the girls' appetites faded fast, but the guys can eat. It was almost time for Young's birthday surprise. With all the food that we ate, we all knew that there was no room in our stomach for birthday cake. We all kind of sat there in disbelief after this great meal, as we felt that we were 5 pounds heavier then when we first came in. Tara said, "I am good for about a week without food." Katy said, "We will be stopping for doughnuts on the way home because Tara has to have some sweets." Greg said, "You better tell Ken to brace Young for the surprise as he spotted the sparklers leaving the kitchen." The staff formed a circle around us, put the cake in front of Young, and The Happy Birthday song began. The staff left and Young blew her stack "Okay wise guys who did this to me?" Steve said, "Ken of course, he just loves playing tricks." The rest of the guys and girls just rolled with laughter. They knew it was probably not Ken, but Steve that pulled the trick. I think Tara and Katy knew Ken really liked Young so this made it even funnier. Ken in his best Jackie Gleason hummena hummena imitation said, "It was not me Young they got me the last time we went out." Greg said, "The

9

moral of the story is to go to the bathroom before going to the restaurant, otherwise it could be your birthday any month of the year." Steve put it in funnier terms, "The longer you pee the more birthdays there will be." "That's not funny Steve," said Young, but then she started to laugh with them. Katy said, "It looks like baby sister Melanie might be next sometime soon." They all laughed with Tara saying, "That girl can hit the can for hours on end." Katy asks, "They ever get you Steve?" "Well I was a little sick and stayed too long in the can at Henries' once but that shouldn't count." "It counts," said Greg who got it at Leon's with a Paczki yet, cakes went fast in that place. Tara said, "Thanks Steve for the great food I'm glad that you're rich." Ken said, "It's not him it's his dad. I worked once as a caddie but I did not last long. The golfer asked me where they hit the ball and I said why would I watch that with all the foxes on the 3rd green? Our paper routes were just to get illegal fireworks, kids stuff." Katy said, "Where did you work Greg?" Greg said, "I mostly worked for my Uncle Leo, he was a cool guy. He owns the best fast food drive-in restaurant in South Chicago." Ken said, "Steve I could go for an angel chicken sandwich and popcorn shrimp now." Young said, "After all the stuff we just ate!" Tara said, "A little bag of popcorn shrimp for the road sounds good." Katy said, "Forget it just the doughnuts and we're done. We are not looking for Leo's tonight." Greg said, "That's alright it's too late anyway, he closed already. I guess we should all go home." Young gave Ken a kiss and said, "Thank you Steve for dinner." Katy not to be out done gave Greg a long kiss, and I suspect a little tongue. Tara said, "Good night Steve," but it was almost like they needed a hotel room. They all said, "See you in class tomorrow." I think the guys went home in a daze, because they did not say much on the ride home. They just had that stupefied look on their faces. When the girls got home and before they went to sleep, they compared their kisses with the guys' and laughed a lot.

The Hunks; Jim, Wayne, Steve, Greg, Stan, and Casey

Act 4

The Axle

IT was a Friday night in the dog days of summer. Steve said, "Let's go have some fun and roller skate our honey's down to the Axle in Niles." Ken said, "That is great for you because you do not fall down all the time like me." Greg also spoke up and said, "I am just average not a pro like Steve, but we got good girls let's suck it up and do it for them." They all agreed and Greg was to make the call since his honey was in charge of everything those girls could do. Greg calling the girls' house, "Hi is Katy there?" "Yes this is Young; I will get the dripping 100LBS princess." "Young you shouldn't have told Greg I just got out of the shower," said Katy. "Why Katy you don't want a naked vision of yourself dancing in his head. Well I guess that could be a good thing," said Young. "Hi Mister Greg," said Katy. "Hi Katy would you Tara, and Young like to go with us guys to the axle for some skating fun tonight? After that we could go to Barnaby's for some pizza or cheese pubs, and some brews. Except no brews for the designated drivers," said Greg. "I love to skate. Let me ask the rest of the girls if they want to go. Young do you what to go skating with the guys tonight at the Axle?" Katy asked. "Yes of course girl and me and Ken are going to smoke you and Greg," said Young. "Dream on Young. Tara is outside washing the car with Melanie. Young go get her and tell her I want to talk to her," said Katy. "I am not doing that Katy. But then Young yells out to Tara, do you want to go to the Axle Roller Dome to go roller skating with the guys?" Young realizes her mistake as Melanie asks, "Can I go too? I am the best skater in the house anyway." Tara said, "Sure Melanie you can go but now its 3 guys and 4 girls. It's not much fun watching little sister. Hey Greg they all said yes but, Melanie wants to come. Young let the cat out of the bag." "That's no problem I'll call Ken's cousin Wayne. He is about her age. So Katy

I will pick you up at 6 pm. Bye sweetie. Ken give your cousin a call to see if he will go," said Greg. "Sure Greg anything to help you to get lucky tonight," said Ken. They all laugh and say, "So we all get lucky." The night had come and they were going in Steve's Electra to pick up the girls. They got there in about 15 minutes. Steve went up to see whether they were ready, because he drove too fast. Let him take the rap if they get mad. Melanie answers the door. He said, "Hey momma you're looking good. If you want to you can borrow my skate key anytime." Hi Steve do you really think I look good?" Melanie asked. "Yes girl, now do a slow turn so I can take in the whole effect," said Steve. "Why she is doing this? What the heck are you doing?" big sister Katy asked. "A slow turn for Steve he said I look great," Melanie answered. "He says that to all the girls. You better stop acting up or you will not go," Katy said. "Big sisters are a big fat pest," Melanie whined. "Okay Steve how come you guys are here so early? Did you drive too fast? Well since you're here go get some coffee and doughnuts. I already told you how I fix my coffee and what doughnut I want, and you better get mine right or I will tell Tara about your little play on my sister. And leave Greg behind. I have to talk to him a little before we go," said Katy. "You got it your majesty," said Steve as he bowed to Katy. Steve went back to the car and told Greg that Katy wanted to talk to him. Greg went up the stairs onto the porch where Katy greeted him with a long passionate kiss. They finally came up for air and Greg said, "Was that for because Steve drives too fast?" She laughs and says, "I guess I have been thinking about you a lot lately. With everyone inside the house we are free to be ourselves." They stay on the porch, talk and smooch thinking no one was watching. Melanie was peeking out the living room window envying her every move. I think she has a little puppy love crush on Greg. They finally stop kissing and talk about how they are starting to really like each other. The silence is broken too quickly. Tara calling down the stairs asks, "Where are those guys with the doughnuts?" Katy said, "There goes our quiet moment I better finish getting ready." They all finally were ready to leave but still no word from Wayne yet. Steve and Tara got into the front seat of the Electra, with Ken and Young in the back seat. Katy is driving the Impala with Greg in the shot gun seat and Melanie in the back seat. Melanie stared at Greg the whole trip there a real stalker. Ken and Young were doing some heavy kissing of their own on the ride there. Tara and Steve where glued next to each other thanks to the beach chair. Katy talked and Greg listened to her on the way to the roller rink. When they got there the place was jumping. The girls had their own skates, and the guys rented theirs. Wayne finally called and said the battery went out on his Vega. He was in Antioch at Hageman's getting a new one put in. He said he'll make it so hold down the fort. The first song was an all skate to Glen Campbell's "Rhinestone Cowboy." Boy that Melanie could fly. Katy was pretty good too. Steve and Tara got all the style steps. Greg was good, and Young and Ken were a work in progress. The next song was a Fox Trot, "Love Will Keep Us Together" by The Captain and Tennille. Katy skated over to the side. Greg stopped alongside of her and asked her what was wrong. She said, "Shit my knee is killing me." Greg said, "I have some Tylenol if you want to take some. We can go take a break and get some nachos. It will still be fun." Katy said, "I do not want to be a party pooper. I think I'll just rest in the snack bar until I feel better. Keep an eye on Melanie for me. She is kind of wild, just until Wayne shows up." Greg said, "I think she has this puppy love thing for me." "I can totally see that but be strong during this test. Do not let her run the show," said Katy. Tara and Steve stopped by to ask what was wrong with Katy. Greg told them her left knee hurt badly. She was going to sit it out for awhile. Melanie was slick and had Greg skating the rest of the night with her, much to the dismay of Katy. Tara came by to talk to Katy saying, "Do you want me and Young to tie her up and put her in the trunk?" "Ha-ha. I can almost say yes to that right now. I told Greg to watch her not to entertain her. Where is this Wayne dude at anyway? That little show off did a couples only skate with Greg," said Katy. It was to the song "Wildfire" by Michael Murphy.

Tara went back to Steve to skate the reverse skate song "Jive Talkin'" by the Bee Gees. Young and Ken took this one off and stayed and talked to Katy who said that her knee hurts badly. Young said, "Maybe we should skip Barnaby's tonight." Wayne finally showed up and he took Melanie off of Greg's hands. He came over to talk with Katy and asked "How is the Tylenol doing is it helping?" Katy said, "Not really and you giving my sister all that attention isn't either. I am sorry Greg. I know the way she ropes people in doing what she wants all the time. I know you could pass this test you're nice. Greg calls Steve over and says, "Hey why don't you take everyone to Barnaby's and Melanie can go with Wayne in his car? I am taking Katy home because she still feels bad. Is that okay Katy?" "Yes sure if you can trust Wayne," said Kathy.

Greg said, "He is cool we should worry about Melanie she's the one with all the ideas." Katy and Greg left for her house and the rest stayed skating a little longer. Greg drove Katy's car and when they got to the house he helped her up the stairs. Katy took some strong pain killer; Advil to help with the pain. Greg said he could give her a full body massage. She agrees and strips naked under a sheet. He was very good at it and soon Katy invited him to bed. He stripped down and slept next to her cradling her all the time. Katy was in heaven with her knight in shining armor. The rest of the group went on to Barnaby's played movie hangman and got some pizza and cheese pub burgers. They had a great time. Young was the first to spot Greg and Katy sleeping together in a spooning fashion. She whispered to Katy that they were back, and she would keep the rest of them busy. Young did a great job and kind of envied Katy's romantic night. The couples kiss each other goodbye and then said goodbye to the rest of the group. Greg came down the stairs kind of punchy and so much in love with Katy.

Katy and Tara

Act 5

Rob Roy

Steve said to Ken and Greg, "Its Friday let's ask the girls to go to the disco "The Rob Roy." "That's a great idea," Greg said. Ken said, "Okay but it's not the 1950's music that I like very much." Steve says, "It's not the music its being with the ladies my man." Steve said, "I'll give Tara a call and set it up. Then let's make it out to the "Rob Roy." They've got a band and a DJ room there." As Steve is calling Tara he says, "Hi! Momma! How is it going? Would you and the ladies want to go to the disco with me and the boys? It'll be my treat." Tara asks Katy and Young and they said it is cool and to pick them up at 8 pm. Greg can drive Katy in her car. They picked them up at 8 pm like they said, but Tara was the slow one that was not ready yet. Katy says, "Tara you look styling in your yellow halter top, green bell bottom pants, gold choker necklace and gold hoop earrings." Tara says, "I know and you Katy, my little lady look sexy in that plum wrap around dress, gold cross and pink opal birthstone earrings. Young said, "Hey! What about me in my silver disco ball mini dress with my Silver Star necklace and matching star earrings?" Tara says, "You always look sharp but we have to work at it Young." "I still like to hear some praise too, so don't leave me out," Young said. Katy came out first, and Greg and her leave, getting an early start on the rest of them. Steve says, "Don't worry Greg drives like an old man. Ken we will catch up to them, even though they had a head start." Tara and Young come out. Steve says, "Look at those foxy ladies." Both Young and Tara laugh. Ken says, "Young you've got some nice legs, you should've wore a mini dress." Young says to Ken, "Aren't you a sweetie." So off they went in Steve's car. Steve turns on the radio and "Sister Golden Hair" by America was playing. They all started to sing along to the tune. Steve pulled up to the Rob Roy in Flossmoor, and not long after Greg pulled up next to him. Katy had been telling Greg how bummed out Melanie was that she was too young to go. Greg thought he was happy that she could not go giving them more privacy on the way home. Maybe a trip to beer can alley was in their future. The club was really jumping with a live band in one room and a DJ in the other room. We got a table close to the dance floor in the live band room where Jinx was playing. They were just setting up when we got there for the first set, doing their testing one, two, and three..... Etc. The first song was, "Why Can't We Be Friends" by War. We all hit the dance floor, what a jam. After it finished, Greg and Ken went to get us all drinks while Steve gave the girls' one of his far out stories of his club experiences. Ken met one of his old girlfriends Sharon. She was a waitress there. "Hi! Sharon, said Ken. Are you still going out with Dennis that ganger?" Sharon said, "No he went to jail for armed robbery. Hey! Ken you seeing anyone now?" "Yes I met a nice looking Korean girl named Young. I met her at Northwestern University," said Ken. "That's good for you, we never had a chance you and me," says Sharon. "No, said Ken we did have a chance but I was not cool enough for you. That's in the past now." "Your right Ken I have never known when to see the good guys, and you were the best," said Sharon. "Well you take it easy, and I hope that you find another good guy. I am hooked on Young, so we don't have a chance now. Goodbye Sharon," said Ken. Greg said to Ken, "What was that all about?" "I used to date her when you were in Nam," said Ken. "Wow! She is a hot momma," said Greg. "She has no soul; I'll take Young every time so let's drop it okay." "Sure Ken, you have your reasons," said Greg. "Let's see Singapore Sling for Young, Long Island Ice Tea for Tara, Tom Collins for Katy, Seven and Seven for Steve, a Heineken for Greg, and Rum and Screwdriver for me," said Ken. As we started drinking our drinks, the band played "Brick House" by the Commodores. We love that song and went to dance to it on the packed dance floor. The song was finishing, and we were going to sit down when the band began playing "The Hustle" by Van McCoy. We of course stayed for that song, and Katy in her plum wrap around dress was spinning like a top showing a lot of black Friday panties. It was a good thing she did not go commando. Greg and Katy took a break and went outside to kiss a little. Or was Greg trying to cool off his Mediterranean goddess from flashing the crowd, who were looking for sure. The break was over for Katy and Greg as they were coming back in. Steve and Tara were going outside to do some kissing of their own. Poor Young and Ken had to hold down the fort at the table, while the others got their friends with benefits. Just as they got back, the band started playing "When Will I Be Loved" by Linda Ronstadt. Ken said to Greg, "Now you and Katy watch our table. Our drinks are coming, and Young really likes this song and wants to dance." Greg said, "Sure go ahead." Ken sure got close to Young on that song. They were starting to get very cozy with each other. When the song ended, Ken and Young went outside to do some kissing too. When Ken and Young came back in, they were all finally seated together at the table with the others. Sharon who somehow ended up being their waitress brought the next round of drinks that they ordered. Romance was in the air, and when Ken and Young looked at each other they both knew that whatever feelings Ken had for Sharon were over. The next song was "Killer Queen" by Queen and every guy in the place was singing along. Soon the girls joined in, and the drinks had finally kicked in and they rocked the song home. The next song was a slow one called "Chevy Van" by Sammy Johns. Everyone stayed on the dance floor for that one. Greg thought that Steve and Tara looked like two people melded together as one. Could two people get any closer? The next song was "Get Down Tonight" by K.C. and the Sunshine Band. This is a song that you dance the bus stop to. Greg said that he needed a break because he hates bus stop songs so he and Katy sat this one out. This was Katy's chance to find out what went on between Ken and Sharon the waitress. Greg asked, "How did you know anything?" "It must be ESP, I guess we girls always know," said Katy. "There is not much to tell they were high school sweethearts. After high school Ken went to college at DePaul downtown, and Sharon just hung out at the old high school. "The Canteen," the school store is where she ran into a real tug named Dennis. He even worked Ken over one time, but Ken got in some good shots though. Ken gave up when she chose him. Now he is in the Joliet pen for armed hold up. I think she knows she messed up, and is trying to break up Ken and Young," said Greg. Katy said, "Do not worry that bitch is not going to hurt my girl." "I'm glad you feel like that, because Ken really digs Young and he is not going to take Sharon back," said Greg. A few drinks later and the song "Long Tall Glasses" came on by Leo Sayer. Ken and Young had practiced a special dance to this song. They were a hit with the crowd, and everyone let them have all the dance room that they needed. Ken and Young came back all tired out. They took a break, while the rest of us danced one more song.

It was "Shining Star" by Earth, Wind and Fire. Sharon tried one more time to bug Ken, but he ignored her. Young said, "You and her have history, yes." "Yes we did, but she flat out left me. You are much prettier and a nicer person. Do not let her bother you. I think I love you," said Ken. Young said, "I think I love you too. Maybe we should leave when the others come back from the dance floor." Young asks Katy, "Can Ken and I take the car, and you and Greg can go back with Steve?" Katy says, "Sure Young." Katy tells Greg about the switch. Steve overhears and tells Greg, "You think we should give Ken a map to Beer Can Alley? Too bad Greg, I guess its breakfast at Denny's for us four on me, and a hot night for Ken and Young at the alley." They all said goodnight to Ken and Young and left. By the way, Ken knew where Beer Can Alley was. Sharon had showed him many years back.

Katy and her Friends from Work

Act 6

The South Side Hit Men

It was a nice Tuesday night for a baseball game. Greg bought us all great seats behind the third base dugout. He got us 8 seats together. Wayne and Melanie came with us this time. Melanie was being a good girl lately by not bugging Katy too much. Wayne had connections with his Dad who got us the good seats. He worked in the office of Bill Veck, the owner of the team. We could not wait for the south side hit men to take the field on that hot August night. They were playing against the Mariners and Gary Wheelox was pitching. We had Steve Stone pitching for us. The girls went for nachos and I sent Steve for the Falstaff Beer. Ken went for the dogs. Wayne went for the pops. I held down the fort from seat stealers. Harry and Jimmy were giving the line ups and Mary and Lorn kept putting their 2 cents in on the radio, channel WMAQ 670. I brought my portable radio with me because I like to listen to the pre-game banter. I had finished getting the score card filled out when they finally all got back to the seats. The top of the first inning started off bad. Stone gave up a homer with one man on base. We were kind of bummed out because we wanted to be the ones hitting the homers. The bottom of first turned out great. Chet got a homer and we got 5 runs that inning. The scoreboard was now going off and the group was happier than ever. Even Steve an incognito Cubs fan was up on his feet cheering with the rest of us. Katy bugs some passerby to take a group picture of us at the top of the second inning. Stone settled down and we got more runs in the 3rd inning. There was a homer by Oscar, a solo shot. Then Eric hit a homer with one man on, and when Jim came up to bat he hit a solo shot homerun. Now we got 4 more runs and the score is 9 to 2 White Sox. We ate some Pro's Pizza during the 5th inning, and we sent Steve and Tara to go get them. They went when the Mariners were batting; there were

8 pizzas in all. Steve and Tara took kind of long coming back. Much to Katy's disdain she said, "I bet those two are smooching somewhere and we have to starve in the meantime." Ken said, "Pizza takes long to cook." Just then they got back, and the first thing Tara asks Young is "Can I use your lipstick?" Katy said, "I knew they were smooching." The 5th inning we get 2 more runs on Eric's second homerun with one on base making the score 11 to 2 White Sox. Stone gives up a triple to Myers in the 6Th inning, and he scores making it 11 to 3 White Sox. The new guy Royle Stillman gets a homer with one on off of Segui in the seventh inning. What a game! 6 homers so far with the score now 13 to 3. Then LaGrow came in to pitch to save the last 2 innings for Stone's win. Steve had little time to make fun of the White Sox's Sailor white uniforms. They have big collars and old time script on them with Chicago in navy blue written on them. Wayne said, "Why did they ever change from the white with black pinstripes uniforms from the 1959 White Sox?" Ken said, "How can you ever forget those white with red pinstripes uniforms. They looked like the Phillies." Melanie said, "I thought that girls were the only ones who care about clothes." Greg said, "This is important. We do not want to be the laughing stock of baseball. Steve at least you guys got rid of those stupid shorts they used last year." Ken said, "One game big deal." The game is almost over and Steve asks Greg to take everyone home in Katy's car. Then he could pick up his Rambler and go home if Katy wants him to. Steve laughs and winks at Katy. Steve said, "A gentleman never says, but I heard you got a hot date with Tara." "That will be the day Steve. You got yourself a deal but you got to let me test out your sunglasses but at night time. I will give them back to you next week," said Greg. "I think that it will probably be years, but what the heck okay," said Steve. The game finished the final score 13 to 3 White Sox. "What a great game, and what good food. I was wondering if it would be any good on a Tuesday night," said Young. "Hey Katy I am leaving to see Steve's Lake Point apartment. Don't wait up for me mother hen," Tara says and then laughs. Then they split up into two groups, and Tara and Steve go back to his place. "It is a nice night with a full moon. I hope that Steve is not a werewolf. I think that is what Tara is looking for," said Young to Katy as they both laugh. Steve turns up the charm and puts on a Barry White album, and opens the drapes with a great view of the lake. Tara says, "You know what I like," and the kissing begins. They start getting busy and the next morning wake up in each other's arms, with a nice sunrise on their faces.

Steve Key

Act 7

Ring at the Fountain

Katy calls Greg and asks "Do you and the rest of our supper club want to go to the movies to see Star Wars at the Esquire Theatre at 7:00 pm on Friday night?" Greg says, "As long as we lose the others after the show. I am with you Katy." Katy says, "Pick me up at 6:00 pm, and have Steve and Ken pick up Tara and Young in Steve's car at that time also." After they hang up the phone Greg gets an idea to ask Steve to call Tara to help him pick out an engagement ring at Albert's on Wednesday, before Katy goes to school. You see he is falling head over heels over Katy, and wants to marry her. He is thinking of asking her on Friday night after the movie at Buckingham Fountain downtown. He also plans on getting Steve to take the rest of the group to Henries', so they do not get in the way of his proposal. I guess I will just have to keep my custom lobster bib in my pocket. Just then Ken rings the doorbell of Greg's Dad's house in the Bush on 8408 Brandon Avenue. Greg tells Ken his plan to ask Katy to marry him, and about going to the restaurant without them. "Just come Greg, to the restaurant after she says yes. I know you want to use your lobster bib," Ken says laughing. Greg says, "Do you think she'll say yes?" "Of course she will say yes. We have been betting on this for about a month now. If you wait one more week I win. That will make you the third one of the original Hunks bowling team who bit the dust because of getting married too soon. First it was Stan and Peggy, then Justin and Maria, and now you. I guess we will not be seeing you around that much anymore," said Ken. Greg said, "Don't be a wise guy we will still hang out." "I am just hassling you about getting married; it will be great," said Ken. "I'd better call Steve, I need Tara to help me pick out the ring," said Greg. Ken says, "What about Young?" "She can't keep a secret till Friday. She will be giggling all the time," said Greg. "I guess you're right," said Ken. "Steve! Are you going to be able to get Tara to help me pick out an engagement ring on Wednesday for Katy?" asks Greg. "Well the big guy is getting up the nerve to ask Katy to get hitched. I am just messing with you. It's cool man, but you are breaking up the bowling team. You're a good bowler, not like Justin and Stan. I have to work on Tara to tell Katy to let you go bowling," said Steve laughing. Steve then left and went to pick up Tara. He got to their place and Young answered the door. Young said, "Hi! Steve. You want me to call Tara?" Steve said, "Yes, but if I can go up and catch Tara just getting out of the shower, that would make my day." "Ha! Ha! Steve, just stay here while I go get her," said Young. Tara came down and away they went. Steve said they were going to pick up Greg and go to Southlake Mall in Merrillville, Indiana. Tara said, "Why didn't he just come with Katy? She was coming home soon from Dunkin' Doughnuts with some good stuff; coffee and doughnuts." "I think I'll let Greg explain it Tara," said Steve. They pick up Greg and take the Skyway to the Indiana toll-way to I-65 getting off at an east exit to Southlake Mall. Tara was getting a little mad at Steve and Greg for not saying anything, but when they went into Albert's the light went on. Tara knew it was about Katy but she put Steve on the spot just for fun. Tara asked, "Steve do you want to get married?" "I say yes," said Tara freaking Steve out. Steve said panicky, "No you got this wrong Tara. Greg wants help picking a ring out for Katy. He is going to ask her to marry him on Friday evening after the movie when they ditch us." "Calm down young man, Tara said to Steve. I figured it out when we walked into the store." Tara looked at a lot of rings and finally said to Greg pointing them out to him, "Here they are! These are the ones." They have a full caret diamond in the center, with two diamonds one on either side in the band. They also come in a set that have the men's and women's wedding band in it. The set costs $3,600.00, and she happens to know Katy's ring finger size is 6. I guess it's a girl thing that they all know each other's ring sizes, and are ready for such occasions. Greg and Steve say it looks like a cool ring, and they will just put the wedding bands part of the set on layaway in case she says no. Steve also says he will front the $1,500.00 to Greg to buy the engagement ring, and a $100.00 down to hold the rest of the set. He knows that Greg is good for it, and that he has been saving money. He has $3,000.00 saved during his 3 years in the Army. Tara is very happy and told Greg, "I know Katy will say yes." Greg said, "I hope that I do this right. I am not as slick as Steve here." Tara said, "You'll do great, and I will not tell Katy or Young. By the way does Ken know?" "Yes Ken knows,

I ran it by him first before I called Steve," said Greg. "I bet Ken asked you why you did not pick Young to do the shopping," said Tara. "Young cannot keep a secret, and she will start giggling and Katy will ask her why and she will spill the beans," said Greg. "I guess we know our Young pretty good," said Tara. "We all better get back, we got school tonight," said Steve. "You're right honey but, you have to get me an angel steak, popcorn shrimp and a strawberry shake from Leo's. You made me miss out on the Dunkin Doughnuts," said Tara. "You got it," said Steve. "Do you want something Greg?" said Steve. Greg said, "I'll have an order of wing dings and fries, and a chocolate shake." After they ate they went to meet the rest of the group at school. Friday was suddenly upon us and we all met one another like we said, downtown. The movie theater was old, and Steve made the comment, I thought I seen a rat reference, which got them all instant hugs of fright from the girls which was the plan. They pretty much stayed close in the hugging position for the rest of the movie. They all agreed that this movie Star Wars was the best movie of the year that they had seen. They did not like that stupid movie that they had seen the last time Annie Hall. Greg and Katy said goodbye to the rest of the group, while they went to Henries'. Greg and Katy just walked, and kept walking toward Grant Park. They went to see the Buckingham Fountain change colors. They got there and Katy splashes some water from the fountain with her hand getting Greg a little wet. Greg would have normally splashed Katy back. What Greg did instead was drop to his knee and he said, "Katy will you marry me?" He then opened the box the ring was in, took it out, and waited for her answer. Katy went from a playful girl to a serious woman in two seconds and she said, "Yes I will" as she put on the ring. Katy said, "It is so beautiful and it fits perfectly. How did you do that?" Greg just said, "Tara and Steve helped me on Wednesday before school. Katy you're going to love the rest of the set." "I just love you right now," said Katy, and as they kissed the fountain turned blue. Greg then said, "I love you too Katy," and they kissed again and the fountain turned red. Katy then asks, "How did Tara my friend keep that a secret?" Greg said, "We did not let her tell Young." Katy said, "Good choice I would have gotten it out of her." They just sat at the edge of the fountain staring into the night. Greg said in his hungry voice, "We can give them the good news at Henries'." Katy said, "Let's go," and gave Greg one last long kiss.

Dr. Margaret Telfer

ACT 8

6 BAUM

The morning start was as hectic as last night had been. The romances were now all wide open. Everyone was having fun. It was an early mid-September day on Saturday, and we just had a sun shower. Katy woke up in intense pain in her left big toe. She could barely stop crying because of the pain. Greg stayed overnight and asked her what was wrong. She said, "It hurts worse than any pain she ever felt before." Greg said, "I have been kind of worried about you. You look so pale. I think we should go now to the ER at Reese and check it out." The troops began to rally and Katy, Melanie, Tara, Steve, and Greg went to the ER. Young and Ken stayed behind. They got to the ER and ran some blood tests. The blood tests came back bad, but this one in particular came back bad with a white blood cell count of 700. They said that Katy had to be admitted to the hospital. A bone marrow aspiration had to be done as soon as she got into her room. Katy held on to Greg, and Tara was comforting Katy by making jokes and trying to keep it light. Steve was parking the car. They were headed to 6 Baumgartner plaza on the sixth floor. Katy's nurse was named Johnny. She was very friendly and tried to calm everyone one down. Katy asks Greg, "What could it be I have never been sick like this before?" Greg said, "I don't know it seems too unreal to figure out what it is." He was a medic and he suspected that it was Leukemia but he just couldn't tell Katy. Tara said, "Just hang in there Katy you'll see you will be fine." They came to do the bone marrow aspiration so everyone had to leave the room. The bone marrow tech was a very big and husky looking man. He used her left hip and when he stuck the needle in, it went so smoothly and fast. It was all over in a half hour. The results would not be back until Monday at the earliest. Greg and Tara went back into Katy's room along with Steve

29

who had finally joined them now to give Katy comfort. It was a rough weekend and they left the hospital at 8 pm when visiting hours ended. Ken, Young, Greg and Melanie came to visit Katy again on Sunday. The doctor came in while they were there with the results from the bone marrow aspiration. The doctor's name is Margaret Telfer. She is very nice, and asked Katy if she wanted her guests to stay during her consultation with Katy about the results. Katy said it was okay for her guests to stay and introduced them to Doctor Telfer. The doctor sat next to Katy who was sitting up at the edge of the bed and held her hand. She said, "I'm sorry dear it's bad news. You have AML Leukemia." Katy started to cry which had the doctor and everyone else with tears in their eyes. Katy pulled herself together and said, "Doctor tell me what I can do to beat this." The doctor said, "First we have to be aggressive and start Chemotherapy as soon as possible. It is called the Introduction stage." Greg said eyes still watery, "Does it always work to kill the cancer cells in the blood and bone marrow?" The doctor said, "Yes it has great results, but the bone marrow transplant will have to be done, after we kill the AML. It is the best course of action for a long term cancer free life. Katy we have to test your whole family to see if we have a match for the bone marrow. That is the critical thing in all this." Katy said, "I have one sister Melanie, and two brothers Tom and Jim, and my parents. Aunts and uncles do not count right?" The doctor said, "That is right it has to be a match from either your brothers or sister, or from your parents. Katy said, "My younger sister Melanie is here today." The doctor said, "Good then we can test Melanie today. Get your brothers and your parents to come in as soon as possible so that they can be tested also. Melanie said, "They are both at home in Cleveland with my Mom and Dad. I will do anything to help my big sister starting today." The doctor asked Katy, "Since your brothers and your parents aren't here can you call them and tell them what is going on? Tell them to go to the Cleveland Clinic to be tested for the bone marrow. After you talk to them, then I will call the Cleveland Clinic to be expecting them. Katy asked Melanie, "Can you call home and tell them what is happening to me and about the test?" "I will call right now," said Melanie. Doctor Telfer said to Katy, "You have to go to surgery tomorrow. You have to get a Hickman double lumen in your chest. We have some great surgeons here. I know this is going so fast, but if you are going to beat this we have to get started right away." Greg said, "Don't worry Katy with God and your family and friends by your side you will beat this." Young said, "We will all take turns to come and see you and bring you food if they let us." Ken said, "You are a great person Katy and you will make it." Melanie got off the phone and told Katy that Mom and Dad started to cry, but their brothers held up and listened to the test instructions. Visiting hours were over and Katy's friends had to leave. Before they left, they all kissed and hugged Katy goodnight. She had to get up early for surgery so she needed her rest. Morning came quickly, and she had a new nurse today. Her name is Carol. Carol said, the gurney was coming and she had to be completely nude under the sheet. The transport guy left her in a line outside the surgery room. One comes out and another one goes in. Katy was freezing her butt off and worried like hell. Please God guide him to do this surgery right, she said to herself. Suddenly it was her turn to go in. She was put on a mechanic table, which is set to meet the surgeon's build. Everything has to be set up according to his specifications, so that he is the most comfortable one in the room. It was time to give Katy the anesthesia. It hit Katy fast and she was out like a light. After the surgery was finished Katy was sent to the recovery room. When she woke up, she then was sent back to her room. Carol was waiting for her, and telling her that she will be just fine. Katy who is still in a daze looks at the line in her chest on the right side. Katy then fell back asleep. She has been through a lot. That afternoon Greg and Melanie came by with some Dunkin Donuts. They bought her a couple of vanilla long johns, which she likes so much. Greg has some Boston cream doughnuts for himself, and Melanie tries the jelly filled doughnuts. Katy shows them the Hickman line and said, "It did not hurt at all." They could not stay too long because Greg and the rest of the supper club had night school at 7:00 pm. The next day, she was told they were going to start the Chemo. Tara and Young came by to hold her hand and visit. They started the Chemo while they were there. It was called Ara-C (Cytarabine). Katy comments, "It is not so bad." The drug takes time to react, and after one hour she was puking her guts out. Tara got the big pan for her to use, and she called it the puker. Young said, "Hold on girl you will be okay." Katy's day nurse today is a new young girl named Marie. She is a very good nurse. Katy said to Young and Tara, "All the nurses that I had so far have been great." Katy had to drop her courses because she was just too sick. Today about a week into chemo, Katy needed a blood transfusion because her hemoglobin was below 8. Marie was her nurse, and it was about 10 am. All of a sudden her pulse (heart rate) shot up to 150 once the transfusion was started. Marie was quick to stop it, and she changed it to another pint of blood because she had a reaction to the first one per Dr. Telfer's orders. Katy thanks Marie for her quick response to the reaction. Marie said, "When you're the young pup on the block you got to prove yourself." Carol and Christine made sure she knew what to do, but they still picked on her just for fun. They both knew she was becoming a good nurse like them. Since she is the youngster that is why they always kept teasing her. The next day Katy had a little cough, because it was so dry in her room. Carol was her nurse and got her a portable humidifier to make her feel comfortable. Katy thanks her. Carol was the most helpful nurse of all going above and beyond what she had to do, and enjoyed doing it. She would talk to Katy about her fishing trips in the Gulf of Mexico for sailfish. She really loved Greg's dad's homemade dill pickles that he used to send with Greg. After starting chemo the only food that doesn't make Katy nauseous is the outside food from Dunkin Donuts, Arnie's hotdogs, and Arby's roast beef sandwiches that her friends bring her. When the hospital food tray comes into Katy's room, just the smell of the food makes Katy puke. Nurse Christine came into the room and had to change Katy's dressing. It has to be changed every 72 hours. Christine is a tall nurse and had to raise the bed very high to do it. Christine had just finished the dressing when she noticed little red pimples on Katy's left leg. She could tell that Katy had been scratching them. Christine called in the resident to look at the pimples on Katy's leg. The pimples were infected. Katy was put on bed rest, and if she had to use the bathroom, she would have to use the bed pan. She had to take Vancomycin for 10 days to fix the infection. Christine told her anytime you get itchy just ask for Benadryl in the IV form. 50 CC will be like a rush and make you sleep not scratch, which is good for you. Katy said, "I know I should have said something. Can I have some Benadryl now? I can't stand it; my leg is itching too much." Katy got the Benadryl and it felt cool. She felt great and relaxed all at the same time. It was a rush just like Christine had said. She then fell asleep, and needed to rest. The next day Katy went to the bathroom and was caught in a very embarrassing position not being able to get back to her bed. Katy pulled the emergency chain, and Marie came to her rescue. She was her nurse today. Doctor Telfer told Katy to not get out of bed. No more walking to the bathroom until the 10 days had passed, and the leg infection was gone. After the infection in her left leg is gone, Katy will have to go to physical therapy to learn to walk again. That afternoon Ken and Steve came to visit Katy, and brought her an Arby's roast beef sandwich to eat. Steve could not help himself as he tries to make time with Katy's nurse Marie. Katy put a quick stop to that saying, "What about your girlfriend Tara?" Steve's response was, "I was just kidding." Ken says, "That's about par for Steve, although I think he really digs Tara." Katy says, "Okay just watch it buddy." Katy talked about the leg infection, and how long she had been on Chemo already, and how weak she felt. When Katy finished talking, Ken and Steve said that they had to leave. They both said goodnight to Katy and they left. The night nurse Shirley arrived, and came in to take care of Katy. She felt really bad and started shaking, and her white count had dropped to 100. The resident on duty would not give her Demerol to stop the shakes. The nurse gave her 8 blankets but that didn't help either. Katy thought she was going to die. She kept up her courage as she was shaking, and talked to Shirley. Shirley came from the Philippines, and is a very good nurse. She kept Katy talking and giving her hope through a long 8 hours that night. Dr. Telfer came in the next morning and ordered the Demerol for Katy. Katy stopped shaking, and went up to 200 on her white counts after the night time blood draw. Dr. Telfer was upset with the night resident and asked him why he didn't call her, and why he didn't take the necessary action to stop Katy from shaking the whole night. The month was almost over when Katy's counts had gone to 1,000 and her latest bone marrow test had showed the AML cancer was gone. That was great news, but she had at least 4 more chemotherapy's to go, plus a consolidation chemo to go. She would be going home for about 2 weeks, and once her counts were better she would get her second round of chemo. She could not wait to get back to her house with Tara and Young, after being in the hospital for 30 days. Katy went home at least five times and then she was done for 3 months before the transplant. The first round had been won against the battle of AML. Hope it stays gone. Greg, Katy's sister, and all her friends went to the St. Jude Shrine in Our Lady of Guadalupe Church to pray the novena for Katy. I know that God is listening.

Dr. Henry Chan

Act 9

Tower of Reconstruction

It feels good to be home in Cleveland for Katy. Mom's good home cooking is helping to fatten Katy up these last four months. The fun was over though; she was going into the Cleveland Clinic for her bone marrow transplant in the middle of February. The first step was to harvest her sister Melanie's bone marrow. It is a painful procedure. They would have to take 100 chips of bone marrow from her hip 99 times more than they did for a bone marrow aspiration. And that pain Katy knew all too well. Katy had to tell Melanie about this pain, and what was going to happen. Katy started to say, "Hey sis I want to tell you again how much this is going to mean to me and my life." Melanie said, "I have known for awhile and I want to say I would do this a 100 times over to save you big sister because I love you." Katy said, "Thanks I love you too," as tears began to form in each other's eyes. "Let's not let mom and dad see us like this," said Melanie. "Okay you little punk," said Katy as she gave her a hug and a kiss on the forehead. "Alright you big bossy sister, said Melanie as she hugged and kissed her sister back on the side of her head. You better not die on me I wouldn't know what to do without your nagging." They both dried their eyes and went into the kitchen so see mom. Mom knew right away that they had been crying, and she started to cry, when both of them came into the kitchen hugging each other. They were all crying then. When their crying subsided mom said, "Katy you have been through so much already. God will not let you down now, and your sister is a brave little girl. She will save you I am sure of that. Now let's get dinner ready you lazy little girls." They all started laughing at the same time. The next day the bone marrow had been gathered from Melanie. Dr. Henry Chan had discussed the Allogeneic Transplant with Katy, her Mom and Melanie. Katy met her first nurse Abby, on the fourteenth floor in the tower. It is the top floor of the hospital. She said they would start hooking her up to the Fludarabine Chemo in her Hickman as soon as it got mixed and sent up. Katy was scared, but ready to do what it takes to get well. Abby was a very nice nurse. She talked about how she thought Katy would do well and beat this cancer once and for all. Abby left and Katy stared out at Lake Erie. Its dark color looked like doom, but then she looked up at the sky. The sky was blue and the sun was shining brightly. After looking at that she then knew that everything would be alright. Katy was glad to have her family there, but missed Greg and the rest of the group. Abby had come back with the chemo and the long process to good health had begun. Katy did not feel any different from the last chemo, but it was not going to be any fun. Katy had a wig that her mom bought her. It was too hot to wear up there. Instead she decided to wear her Chicago Bear's stocking cap. That was not a popular choice with all the Cleveland Browns fans from there. The second day of her chemo was the same chemo, and she would get it for 2 more days after today's dose is done. Katy's nurse today was Lindsey. She was from St. Louis, and a big Cardinals fan. Lindsey said, "What is up with that Bear's hat? Aren't you from here?" Katy said, "They are the team I like, and my boyfriend likes them." Lindsey said, "Okay let's make a truce. We'll take a walk and see if Carolyn the social worker has some candy. She has a big stash. I'll show you the ropes." On the third day of this chemo her nurse was Cindy. She was a very tall nurse who was very friendly. She had brought her a Chocolate Ensure drink. She tried to pull Katy higher up in the bed, and knocked the bottle of ensure all over her. What a big mess. Cindy kept on apologizing. Katy just laughs and said, "Don't worry you are a good person. You were trying to help me. It can happen to anyone." Cindy said, "All of the nurses are going to laugh at me." Katy said, "Let me talk to them. You are a sweetheart they would not dare say anything." The next day was day four, and it was her last Fludarabine Chemo treatment. Katy's new nurse was Sarah. She came into Katy's room and noticed how weak Katy was from not eating. Katy was puking so much that her lips were all chapped. Sarah is about Katy's height, and was wearing a gray tee shirt and gray Dickies scrubs pants. She gave Katy some crackers and some Vaseline for her chapped lips. She told her to try to eat something, because she needs to stay strong. Katy said, "You're so good to me. I hope that I get well so me and my boyfriend Greg, and you and your husband can go out disco dancing and have some drinks. It would be fun." Day five came and she was going to get Melphalan Chemo for the first time. Now her nurse that day was Erin. She walks with heavy footsteps, so you know that it was her that was coming by how loud her steps were. She is very nice, a real sweet girl who was comfortable to be around, and is easy to talk to. She could almost out talk me, Katy said. It is now day six today and I got my last dose of chemo. Shama is my nurse and she got me an ice cream swirl chocolate malt. We just talked about everything. Day seven arrived and it was time for Campath. Jen is my nurse and she told me that this is a very critical stage. She held my hand as it started and is so kind and caring. It is day 8, and for me it is the day of new birth. I will get Melanie's stem cells. Kristen my nurse said, "The future is now Katy." The nurse pumped Melanie's stem cells into my right side. I feel like Melanie is taking over my right side. "She is not as good a dancer as I am," said Katy as Kristen laughed. The next day her brother Jim and his wife Ann came to see Katy. Jim said, "This is a turning point for you Katy. You will get better." Katy said, "I know you look like Jesus, Jim but it would take a miracle to make me feel better." Ann said, "Keep thinking positive and keep praying to God." Jim says, "Just when you think you can't go on anymore a light comes shining through." Katy said, "It has been so hard for me. I miss Greg and my friends, and I want my life back." Ann says, "It is something that happens that was unexpected, and it happens in the midst of the new day." Jim says, "The kingdom of the future is the strength of the past." Ann said, "We have a letter here from Greg to you Katy." Katy reads. Dear Katy, You're pretty like a lotus blossom or a rose that is blue. For you to be not you is like a heart that doesn't speak the truth. Which is all that you can be is very fine with me. I hope we will be good friends. Good friends pass by slowly, but those that rush past you do not stay long. You will always pass by slowly for the end of time. Katy stops and says, "Lyrics." Katy's nurse today was Connie. She heard part of the letter from Greg, and she asked Katy if she could read it. Katy said, "Sure." Connie thought it was beautiful and said, "He seems like a nice guy." Katy said, "He is a real romantic. The next day Katy had a fever. It was 103.5 F. Her nurse Jennifer brought in ice packs to put under her arms and on the back of her neck. Adriana the PCT, helped move her up in the bed. The ice packs did a good job to help lower the fever. Dr. Chan gave the okay for her to take Acetaminophen and ordered a chest X-ray. The worst was confirmed; Katy had pneumonia in both lungs. Dr. Betty Nguyen the pulmonary doctor was called in and she prescribed the antibiotic Vancomiacin.

The following day Katy's fever went down to 102.5 F. Her nurse Alexi who spoke two languages English and Polish said, "Don't worry you will get well." She said something in Polish which translates, "Hold on to yourself, your heart and God and everything will be okay." That night the night nurse Mora knew that Katy had a rough day. She was able to draw her blood at 1 a.m. without waking her up. She let her get her rem sleep. The next day Katy had to have a bronchoscopy, and they put her under anesthesia. When the anesthesia wore off, she was awakened up by Ricki her nurse that morning. Katy started swinging and talking crazy like she was the queen and everyone else were her knights. Ricki had to get help from Margie to hold her down. They called her brother Tom, and he and his wife Ann tried to calm her down and it finally worked. It took some time, and Katy told Ricki that she was sorry for swinging her hands at her. Ricki said, "That part of the job was new to her and she was not expecting that." Dr. Chan came in and said that it was probably one of the drugs used to put you to sleep. It will be okay now. The pneumonia hung on, and the next day Tori was her nurse. The fever did drop though. Tori said, "I remember when you first came in, and Melanie and your dad brought you a cassette player. After they left you were dancing to "Stayin' Alive" by the Bee Gees. I called Gina the other nurse who was there to watch you dance. You are a good dancer." Katy said, "I know I practice and follow the bass." The next day Katy was feeling better yet and said, "I wish I had some Pizza." Gina her nurse that day said, "We will buy you some pizza. We are ordering out and I know you cannot eat this stuff that they bring you. You are fading away to 88 lbs. That evening Lydia her nurse noticed that Katy's fever began to spike up again. She got the ice packs and put them on Katy and her fever settled back to 101.5 F. The next day it was much better as nurse Catharine saw that her temperature dropped to 100.1 F. and her lungs seemed clearer. Dr. Betty Nguyen came the following day and she did say that Katy was better. Her counts were stable, and she could go home in a few days. Finally that next day she had no fever. Katy had Katie for her nurse and she said, "Let's go do some walking. The following day Corri was her nurse. Katy was happy because she was going home. She had a long road ahead of her with a lot of rehab. She had to build up her strength and gain some weight. She knew that wouldn't be a problem with mom's good cooking. It has been a long and winding road but with God, her family, Greg, and her friends beside her she will make it.

Ken and Justin

Act 10

Cana

Katy was well, and on her way back to Chicago. The plane ride took forever like it always does whether you are departing or arriving to ORD. Katy brought her sister Melanie with her, and promised her a lot of fun gave her a big hug and said thank you to her for the bone marrow donation. Melanie said, "Do I get a drink at the disco with a fake ID?" Katy said, "You know better than that Melanie, but you can still have some fun." "I know I was just messing with you like always," said Melanie. Katy said, "I cannot wait to see Greg." "I can't wait to see Wayne. Maybe we can find the beer can alley," said Melanie. "You better not little sister," said Katy. Greg was there with Ken and Young to welcome them at ORD. Tara and Steve were holding a table for them all at "Pop N' Fresh Pies." Greg and Katy had a long kiss and hug for each other. Ken and Young took Melanie and went to get the luggage. The two lovebirds were walking slowly hand in hand as if they would never be alone again. Finally they show up at the B12 baggage carousel. Katy hugs and kisses Young and Ken and says hello. Young said, "I thought that you would never stop kissing us." Katy said, "That is not all that I plan to do." Ken said, "It is great to see you both again Katy and Melanie. Katy you're so skinny now." "I know that chemo diet again," said Katy. Greg said, "Let's get to the restaurant. There is a lemon meringue pie waiting for you Katy with your name on it. An apple pie is there waiting for me." Ken said, "I got to go with the blueberry pie." Young said, "Its cherry pie for me all the way." Melanie said, "Its pumpkin pie or nothing for me." They came to Sibley Boulevard in Dolton to the restaurant and there was Steve and Tara eating up their two pieces of strawberry pie. Steve and Tara had two pieces of the peach pie too. Steve and Tara kissed and hugged their friend Katy, and welcomed her back to Chicago. Wayne showed up and he got some custard pie. Katy kept a big sister eye on him and Melanie. Tara asked, "Why the watchful eye on little sister Katy?" "I think she is growing up too fast that's all," said Katy. "Now Katy what about these wedding plans," said Young. "I guess grey tuxes for the groomsmen, and purple dresses for the bridesmaids," said Katy. "How about David's Bridal in Oak Lawn?" Young asked. "That is cool," said Katy. "What do you think about 6 groomsmen and 6 bridesmaids?" Tara asked. "That sounds perfect," Katy said. "Who is going to be the maid of honor? Me I hope," Tara said. "Without a doubt it has got to be my sister Melanie. There would be no me without her. "Besides you and Young would have to fight it out, and I cannot let you do that," Katy said. Young said, "Good choice Katy, I did not become second best friend again." "I know Greg wants Justin as his best man," said Katy. "I thought that he is married to Maria," said Tara. "We will have six bridesmaids including the maid of honor, and six groomsmen including the best man. We invite Maria as a bridesmaid to stand up with Wayne. And Justin will stand up with Melanie. After the church ceremony Melanie will go back to Wayne. Justin will go back to Maria," said Katy. "I think you're on to something. Maria is a fashionista and can help us all out. She is also a great dancer, look what she did with Justin. They dance great together," said Young. "Now wait a minute, us sisters can dance too. Maria she knows her make-up and fashions so it's cool," said Tara. "What about Peg and Stan they would bring a lot to the table? Peg is a gas, and Stan has been through this he knows," said Melanie. Katy said, "Okay let's do a head count, Greg and Me, Justin and Melanie, Steve and Tara, Ken and Young, Wayne and Maria, Stan and Peg, that is five we need two more. I have to have my cousin Lindsey MacDowell and I'm sure Greg will want George." Melanie asked, "You mean that rub it in winner, and sorry loser we played Uno with?" "Yes she is a real cover girl now. Who would think that was even possible? Not something you would expect, especially someone from Pekin, Illinois. Now she is a New York cover girl and model," said Katy. "I still don't like her, "said Melanie. Katy said, "She is real cool now. Just you wait and see. She came by to visit us at the house when you were in school two falls ago." Young said, "She was fun and not mean at all." Tara said, "Her clothes were out of sight." "Okay but to be safe let's not play any games with her," said Melanie. The pies and coffee came, and everyone was digging in now. The next day Ken asked, "Hey do you want to go fishing at Wolf Lake?" Greg said,

"I would like to spend more time with Katy." "Bring her with you and we can take the whole gang," said Ken. "I think she might like it. She has been in hospitals for the last 2 years," said Greg. Greg asks Katy if she and her friends and her sister would like to go fishing at Wolf Lake. "I think it would be cool. Let me call you back with their answer. You better make sure Steve and Wayne come also," said Katy. Katy asks Tara, Young and Melanie if they were willing to go fishing with the guys. She asked them if they would help her and Greg ditch the rest of the crew for some sunset kissing at the shoreline. "I got you sister. Let you and Greg have some privacy and watch the submarine races," said Tara. "I am willing to help you," Young said. Melanie asked, "What are submarine races?" "You are too young to know, and Tara is kidding anyway," said Katy. Katy calls Greg back and tells him it's a go, but not about ditching the others part. Ken gets the night-crawlers and minnows with Steve at Val's Bait Shop and they head out to Wolf Lake. Steve said, "I bet its takes them 2 hours to get here." "It will take Greg and Wayne longer than that," said Ken. Ken fishing the old bridge on the east side has caught a 5 lbs. large-mouth bass on minnows and a barber about 4 feet down. Steve fishing the bottom with night-crawlers has caught a 4 lbs. channel cat. Ken has also caught 3 blue gills and 2 croppy. Steve also caught 4 perch and 1 rock bass and 1 sunfish. Greg, Wayne and the girls finally get there. Steve says, "We got all the fish already. Where have you guys and girls been?" "Don't start with us lover boy," says Tara. Katy said to Greg, "Let them go and just hang back here with me. We're never alone anymore." Greg said, "Sure I've been missing you a lot. We need to go for a walk. I bet you're glad to be outside. Katy said, "I am but being with you is the best part of getting well. There were so many times that I wanted to give up, but I have always been a fighter who knows that God would help me." "I'm glad you did," said Greg as they walk north around the lake toward the old Nike Ajax bunkers ground to air missile defense from the Cold War. Katy was amazed by it, and by the fact that no one knew about it. "I think it was top secret, and they did a great job hiding it," Greg said. Greg and Katy then walked ahead east along the lake. Greg said, "It really broke my heart to see you so sick." Katy stopped and kissed with Greg and said, "I knew you were always there in spirit for me, and I knew you would not let me down." They kiss again and Katy said, "What a great letter that you sent me. I think that was the turning point, when I knew that I would make it." "Which one asked Greg?" "I think you know which one," said Katy. "I put my heart into it and I really took the time to say I love you in words," said Greg. Katy gave Greg a French kiss and said, "Let's go back to the car. We have some submarine races to watch." "I hope that I make it to at least third base before Wayne comes along and spoils it," said Greg. "He's just a kid. Give him a break. I know that he asks a lot of questions. He is going out with my sister so do not tell him too much," said Katy. "I hope that they are catching a lot of fish to keep them busy. I am going for home plate," said Greg. Katy asked, "But what if they come back sooner?" "My main man Steve will see the windows and divert them," said Greg. "It sounds like you've been in this situation before. Who was she?" asked Katy. "That is not important. I love you and I always will," said Greg. They were able to finish without any interruption. When they were dressed again the sun was setting. It was beautiful and it meant a new beginning for them both. Greg said, "I hope never to see you sick again. I love you honey." "I hope the AML is history. Thanks to my little sister. She was very brave, and it took a lot out of her. My mom told me how sore and tired she was. She did not complain once. About the pain that I knew she had. I had it only once for her 100 times each bone marrow aspiration donation," said Katy. Greg asked, "She was in the next room?" "Yes the fresher the marrow that they take, the better the chances are," said Katy. The rest of the group made their way back. They had plenty of fish for all of us. Steve said, "You sure missed it. Ken caught a 10 lbs. large-mouth bass. "I guess we were just not into it today," Steve said. Tara asked, "I think we were into it right Katy?" "Shut up Tara you just leave us alone, "said Katy with a laugh. Melanie asks Young, "What are they talking about?" Young said, "In a few years you'll know what we are talking about." Ken said, "Let's go clean these fish." Steve says, "Let's just give them to Tat, Justin's dad. He will clean them and he can have them. He will just be mad that he did not catch them, because he had to work." Tara said, "Steve you promised me fish for dinner." "I have a good idea. Let's go to Arthur Treachers for some fish," said Wayne. Greg says, "That sounds good to me." They drop the fish off at Mr. K's house and head for Treachers or as Tat calls it Creatures. The next day Katy had a slight limp and Young asked "What is wrong?" Katy said, "I hit my big toe on a rock yesterday on the walk Greg and I took around Wolf Lake." Young said, "It looks pretty bad. You should go to the podiatrist. It looks like a hang nail. I had to go to a podiatrist before. I went to Doctor Allen Shoelsun. He is great." Katy said,

"He better be. We have the wedding rehearsals coming up soon." Greg, Katy, and Young go to the podiatrist's office. Greg shows off and carries Katy into the office. Greg then looked at Young and asked "What?" Young said, "You can't wait to practice for the whole threshold thing." They get Katy inside the examination room, and they take her for X-rays. Greg said to Young, "I got a house for us on the east side. It is my wedding present to Katy. Don't tell anyone especially Tara or Melanie. "You better not tell your boys either. They can spill the beans too," said Young. When Katy came back inside the examination room after they finished taking the X-rays, the doctor came in. He told Katy that her toe was not broken. He also told her that she was going to lose her toenail, and that it is infected. Katy asked, "Is there any other choice?" The doctor said, "I can treat it with antibiotics and check it again in one week." Katy asked, "What can I do in the meantime with it?" "I can give you pain pills if that's okay with Dr. Chan, and Clindamycin for the infection. You will have to clean it in a basin with Bernadine twice a day for 3 minutes," said the podiatrist. Katy asked, "You want me to soak it for 3 minutes in what kind of water temperature?" The doctor said, "No I said clean it for 3 minutes in lukewarm comfortable water." Katy asked, "What is the difference between soaking it and cleaning it?" "If you soak it too long it opens you up for more infection. That's why only cleaning it for the 3 minutes," the doctor said. Katy asked, "Do I put my sock back on?" She was wearing gym shoes. The doctor said, "You can put your sock on your foot that is ok. For your other foot I will get you a surgical shoe." He left to go get the shoe and when he came back he wrapped up Katy's toe. He showed her how to do it too. The doctor said, "Okay try the shoe on and see how it feels." Katy said, "It feels great with no pressure on my toe. It leaves my big toe back some so that I won't bump it again." "That is why it's made that way. Okay see you in a week, and do the cleanings," the doctor said. Katy mumbled to herself on the way to the front desk soak, soak, soak. Greg was waiting for her there at the front desk. They both went to get Young. She was reading a People magazine. Greg and Young helped get Katy to the car calling her Chester a few times. Katy was limping because the special shoe the doctor said that she had to wear was lower than her regular shoe that she wore on her other foot. Katy came back in one week to see the doctor with Greg, Young and Tara. This time they used a wheelchair. Katy was getting tired of their Chester jokes. Katy went in the room to wait for the doctor. The nurse told her to sit on the table. Greg stayed in the lobby with Young and Tara. Tara said, "I have to go to the bathroom. Young are you coming?" Greg gave Young a look like he wanted to talk to her. Young said, "No I am good. You go ahead Tara." Greg asked, "You didn't tell anyone about the house?" Young said, "Silly question. If I would've talked, we would've all seen the house by now." "I am sorry Young that I bugged you. I really want this to be a surprise for Katy after all that she has been through," said Greg. "I know Greg that's why I didn't say anything," said Young. Greg said, "You are a true friend thanks. Now stop dancing in your chair, and go to the can. You can sure drink a lot of pop." "I guess you are right. How did you know?" asked Young. "Katy is always going to the can. She lives on coffee. It must be a girl thing," said Greg. "I remember when you were at the game drinking beer. You go a lot too," said Young. Greg said, "You got me there. You better go now so Tara doesn't think that something's up." The doctor finally came in to see Katy. He was in the room next door, with a lady who was screaming for her life. That did not sit too well with Katy. If this hurts I am going to kill Young. Dr. Shoelsun came in and asked Katy to take off her shoes and socks. The doctor then looks at the difference between the two toes and says, "The toe still looks infected and the nail has to come off." Katy asks, "Is it going to hurt?" The doctor said, "I don't know. Last week I was emptying the garbage and someone asked me, do you want to start taking off toe nails on the side for more money? I said yes." Katy said, "I know that trick. Young warned me about you being a joker. You almost had Young crying before you told her the truth doctor." The doctor said, "I'm sorry about scaring your friend." The doctor then told Katy to lean back as he extended the table to lengthen her feet out longer, and lowered the back rest. The doctor then took a long needle and syringe filled with Lidocaine and injected it into both sides of the infected toe. Katy jumped a little, but she didn't scream. The second shot didn't hurt as much. Before she knew it, the doctor had the nail off and Katy felt nothing. He was very good indeed. The doctor was showing Katy how to wrap up her toe and put on the antibiotic cream Mupirocin. The cream was for just in case the nail comes back with MRSA. Making small talk with Katy the doctor asked, "Do you like movies?" Katy said, "Yes my boyfriend and I just went to see the movie Midnight Express. It was very good. It makes you think." The doctor said, "Stop right there. Don't give the plot away. I haven't seen it yet." Katy said, "I'm sorry, I do talk a lot. The doctor said, "You should go see the movie

The Deer Hunter. You and your boyfriend will like that movie. If the toenail has MRSA, I will call you and switch the antibiotics. Come back to see me in two weeks to see if your toenail is getting better." Greg, Katy, and Young left. After 48 hours the results came back from Katy's toenail. The doctor called Katy and told her the results tested positive for MRSA. He told her that she had to take a different antibiotic called Zyvox. He told her that he called in the prescription, and that she should pick it up at Walgreens. Two weeks passed, and Katy went to see the doctor again. This time only Greg went with her. The doctor said, "Everything looks okay now. Just be careful and watch how you cut your toenail when it grows out. If you have any more problems come back to see me again." The doctor asked Katy, "Did you get to see the move The Deer Hunter that I told you about the last time you were here?" Katy said, "Yes it was a very good movie. Christopher Walken is an excellent actor." Katy asked the doctor, "Did you get to see the movie I told you about Midnight Express?" The doctor said, "I think I'll stay away from Turkey for awhile." Katy said, "You're a stoner and laughed." "I guess I had that coming for the way that I bugged you and your friend," said the doctor. "Goodbye see you doctor. You are invited to come to our wedding if you can. We have plenty of girls that are looking for doctors or janitors," said Katy. Katy laughed as she left. The doctor said, "Maybe I will." Katy and Greg then went home to Greg's parents' house. The wedding day approached. Greg and Katy went to St. Michael's church, and met up with their friends, plus everyone who was standing up to their wedding. They had a practice rehearsal before the actual wedding ceremony. After the rehearsal they went to Barnaby's Pub in Calumet City to get something to eat. The singer that they are going to get for the church ceremony is a cousin of Tara's. Her name is Sharon Winfrey. She is a very good singer and sang in her church choir. Katy asked, "What do you all think about the offertory song being "How Great Thou Art?" That is good they all agreed. "What about "You Raise Me Up" for a Communion song," asked Ken? They all said okay to that song too. Young asked, "What about "On Eagles Wings" as the recession song? Katy said, "That is a nice song. We'll use that song as well." Greg asked, "What about "We Are One Body?" Steve said, "I don't like that song." Katy said, "Greg likes it so that song is in too, and that is final." They all laughed because they knew that they weren't going to change Katy's mind. "The flower girl should be my brother Jim's daughter Marley. She is so cute, and is 7 years old the right age," said

Melanie. Katy said, "Yes Marley is in." Then Katy asked, "What about our brother Tom's boy Finn? He is 8 years old. He can be the ring bearer." Melanie said, "If you can get him to sit still. That boy is fast and runs circles around me." Katy said, "Don't worry I'll be there and I'll make him slow down." Greg asked, "What about security at the hall? We have booked the Memorial Hall. I remember meeting Vanessa Houston at Justin and Maria's wedding. She said that she was available for our wedding on September 27, 1980." Katy said, "I remember her. She was real good. She kept your friends in line Steve." Steve said, "Now wait a minute Katy. I was just rapping to this girl. How did I know she had a big boyfriend who could've played for the Chicago Bears?" Ken said, "That was a close one Steve." Katy said, "Yes to Vanessa. She was cool about how to handle the situation." Greg said, "I think Anne MacDowell Lindsey's younger sister is great at crafts. Melanie said, "She can do the party favors, and she is not bossy. I can get Caryn, Kelly and Sabrina to come and help Anne. They are also good at arts and crafts. They make pretty flowers out of tissue paper." Katy said, "I was waiting for you to get your friends involved in this sooner or later. This bone marrow of yours better last Melanie. I'm just kidding." "The flowers are coming from Elizabeth's Floral Shop. I have known her a long time. The cake will be from Calumet Bakery. They make the best cakes there," said Greg. Katy said, "It was nice of Maria to lend us her cake book. That way we could pick out the cake that we like. We then can show the people at Calumet Bakery what we like, and see if they can make the cake that way. What Greg and I decided on was a 3 tier cake with fresh strawberries, whipped cream, half chocolate and half vanilla. Calumet bakery said that wouldn't be a problem, and they would be able to make the cake the way we wanted it. We were very happy about that. The guys got their tuxedoes at Dunhill. They are grey with lavender shirts." Greg said, "The photographer is from Foxes in Oak Lawn, Illinois. They are the best. Stan the man used them and they were great." Katy said, "I think we should have two bands. It would be continuous music and a good variety. One band will play Polish music, and the other band will play disco music. Everyone likes to dance and it will be very enjoyable." The day of the wedding was at hand. It was a beautiful Indian summer day. The temperature outside was 72 degrees. Greg and Justin waited in the rectory, while the bridal party gathered and got set up outside St. Michael's Church. Sharon was in the choir upstairs with the organist getting ready for the entrance song. The priest Father Jim told

Greg and Justin to go to their places near the altar with him and the altar boys. The organist played here comes the bride, and the bridal party slowly walked into the church. It was breathtaking as Katy walked in with her Dad to the altar and he gave her to Greg. The entrance song began and the mass was in progress. Psalm 45 was used and Sharon sang it great, as she did the entrance song. The first epistle of the Old Testament was read by Katy's mom; Deuteronomy chapter 4 versus 35 to 45. Then Greg's dad read Romans chapter 8 verses 28 to 38. Melanie followed by reading the Gospel of John chapter 2 verses 1-12. After the Gospel Father Jim then said the homily. He said, "I am here today to bring Katy and Greg together in marriage. The love that now is new and fun will take many shapes. There will be times of sickness which they already experienced and have overcome. The children that they have will always be number one. The long hours they both will work to pay their bills and support their family. There may be shift changes and layoffs that they have to deal with. I tell you a good heart will overcome all. The patience of Job is also needed. Talking and praying to God will help you get through anything. God will never desert you. Remember God in good times and in bad times. Do this and you will never be sad. He will walk by your side and comfort you when you are in distress and cry. The friends that you both have here today will also give you a hand. The ones that are kind find kindness in return. Greg, be by Katy's side at your children's birth. I know you can take off from work. I think that you see God's great plan to help us continue His love. The thing to do Katy and Greg is to enjoy the time at hand, for only the Father knows all that is planned. Pray to Jesus and ask for the wisdom of the Holy Spirit, for as we were dust we shall return to dust. I leave you with this final thought, never do things for revenge. To forgive is the way of the cloth. It must be the way of your love." "I, Greg, take you, Katy, to be my lawfully wedded wife. I promise to be true to you in good times and in bad, in sickness and in health. I will love and honor you all the days of my life. I will be yours always. Our love will shine until the end of time." I, Katy, take you, Greg, to be my lawfully wedded husband, to have and to hold from this day forward, for better, for worse, for richer, for poorer, in sickness and in health, until death do us part. I love you with all of my heart, for you are my soul mate. I want to spend all the days of our lives happy together. I have been unkind, but not to you my love. You have made me a better person. Always in my heart you will stay." Finn brings the rings to Father Jim to be blessed.

Afterwards Father Jim tells Finn to take the rings to Greg. Greg picks up the ring for Katy and as he puts it on her finger he says, "Katy I place this ring on your finger to tell you again that I love you." Katy and most of the women shed a tear. Katy picks up the ring for Greg and as she puts it on his finger she says, "Greg I place this ring on your finger to tell you again ditto that I love you too." Father says, "You may kiss the bride." Greg lifts up Katy's veil and kisses her with his whole heart. Katy returns the kiss to Greg with her whole heart. The church erupts with applause for they are now married in the eyes of the Lord. Greg's mom now reads the Prayers of the Faithful. She concludes with, "May Katy and Greg have a long and happy marriage. We pray to the Lord." The congregation responds again with, "Lord hear our prayer." The assembly sits. The Offertory Song now starts "How Great thou Art" and Sharon's singing is flawless. The Presentation of the Gifts are brought up by Finn and Marley. Father Jim then says, "Pray, brethren, that my sacrifice and yours maybe acceptable to God, the Almighty Father," The assembly stands. The Eucharistic Prayer begins. Father Jim starts the Preface dialogue. Father Jim says, "The Lord be with you." The assembly says, "And also with you." Father Jim says, "Lift up your hearts." The assembly says, "We lift them up to the Lord. Father Jim says, "Let us give thanks to the Lord, our God." The assembly says, "It is right to give Him thanks and praise."

Father Jim then goes to the Preface (giving praise and thanks to God) using Eucharistic Prayer #II. Father Jim starts by saying, "Father, it is our duty." And he finishes by saying, "Proclaiming your glory." The Holy Holy is next. The assembly says, "Holy Holy and ends with Hosanna in the Highest." We then all kneel. The Epiclesis (calling on the Holy Spirit) is next. Father Jim continues with Eucharistic Prayer #II, "Lord, you are holy indeed and finishes with Lord, Jesus Christ." Father Jim says, "Before he was given up to death, a death he freely accepted, he took the bread and gave you thanks. He broke the bread, gave it to his disciples, and said: Take this all of you and eat it: this is my body which will be given up for you. When supper was ended, he took the cup. Again he gave you thanks and praise, gave the cup to his disciples, and said: Take this all of you, and drink from it, this is the cup of my blood, the blood of the new and everlasting covenant. It will be shed for you and for all so that sins may be forgiven. Do this in memory of me." The Memorial Acclamation was next: sung by all. Christ has died, Christ is risen, Christ will come again.

The Anamnesis, Offerings, and Intercessions followed: In memory of his death and resurrection, we offer you, Father, this life –giving bread, this saving cup. We thank you for counting us worthy to stand in your presence and serve you. And finishes with Mother of God, with the apostles, and with all the saints who have done your will throughout the ages. May we praise you in union with them, and give you glory through your Son, Jesus Christ. The Doxology is next and the Great Amen. Father Jim sings, "Through him, with him, and in him, in the unity of the Holy Spirit, all glory and honor is yours, almighty Father, for ever and ever." We all stand, and sing Amen. Father Jim then says the Communion Rite: followed by the Lords Prayer which we all sing. Father Jim then faces the couple and gives them the nuptial blessing. Father Jim says, "Let us offer each other the sign of peace." Everyone shakes hands, and Katy and Greg kiss each other. Then Katy and Greg shakes the hands of others at the altar and saying to each one, "Peace be with you." The Agnus Dei is sung next in Latin by all. When we all finish singing we all kneel and pray the prayer before we receive communion. We all pray and say, "Lord I am not worthy to receive you, but only say the word and I shall be healed. We beat thy chest as in the Roman days. Sharon beautifully sang the communion song, "You Raise Me Up" while everyone went up to receive communion. After communion we all stand. The Concluding Rite is followed by the Blessing. Father Jim extends his hands over the bride and groom and says, "May God Eternal Father keep you of one heart in love for one another. That the peace of Christ my dwell in you and abide always in your home." Response: "Amen" from Greg and Katy. Father Jim continues and says, "May you be blessed in your children, have solace in your friends, and enjoy true peace with everyone." Response: "Amen" from Greg and Katy. Father Jim says, "May you be witnesses in the world to God's charity, so that the afflicted and needy who have known your kindness may one day receive you thankfully into the eternal dwelling of God." Response: "Amen" from Greg and Katy. Father Jim blesses all the people, adding: "And may almighty God bless all of you, who are gathered here, in the name of the Father, and the Son, and the Holy Spirit." Response: all the people say "Amen." Father Jim says, "Greg you may kiss the bride." Dismissal: Father Jim says, "The mass is ended, go in peace." All say, "Thanks be to God." Sharon starts singing the Recessional song, "On Eagles Wings." Everyone starts walking slowly out of the church. Greg and Katy, the bridal party, the ministers, the altar boys and girls, and

Father Jim. Sharon then sang a special song "Alleluia" as they all walk out. Outside the church Greg had rented a limo and it had on it the just married sign and cans attached onto the back of the car. Casey and his date Dori, had set that all up. When Greg and Katy arrived at memorial hall, Vanessa was going over stuff with Katy's Dad. Greg and Katy greeted everyone as they came inside along with the bridal party. There was an open bar in the back and Greg's friends were already the first in line. Soon Greg's dad was announcing over the PA system, "Let's have a hand for the bride and groom, as man and wife Greg and Katy Krasinski." Then the rest of the bridal party was announced as everyone was clapping. Everyone was there. Casey Kludzinski, Justin's younger brother, brought that good looking redhead from the east side Dori Ewing. She was all decked out in a blue periwinkle low cut short dress. She was definitely a hit. Maria Kludzinski was also a girl getting a lot of looks in her simple black dress. I have to say Lindsey from the bridal party, was another girl that was getting a lot of attention from the guys. Katy and Greg spent most of dinner kissing, with people banging their spoons on their glasses. It was time now for Justin's speech, with a toast to Katy and Greg. Before he could even start Danny, Tim and Mark said, "We want to eat so cut it short." They knew how long winded Justin can be. Justin said, "I just want to say I am so happy for Katy and Greg. May they have a long and happy life together. Now let's get this party started Na zdrowie!" They all clanked their champagne glasses in their toast for Greg and Katy. The food was being served. It was family style, homemade Polish sausage, Italian beef, fried chicken and mostaccioli. It is the best food on the east side of Chicago. When everyone had finished eating the music and dancing had begun. Greg and Katy danced their first dance together. It was a slow Viennese waltz. Then everyone from the bridal party joined in. And the guests joined in also. Justin switched dancing partners with Wayne. Wayne was now dancing with Melanie, and Justin was dancing with Maria. The Polish band was playing now, and when they were on their break the DJ took over. They were switching back and forth like this. That was good because there was continuous music playing so everyone could enjoy themselves and keep on dancing. Joanne was a friend of Katy's from Cleveland, Ohio. She was dancing with Justin's Godfather Mieczyslaw Kludzinski. He was a very nice guy. Caesar came in with his girlfriend, who Greg and Katy met at a Santana concert. Bridget came with her boyfriend Sam. Mark was there with his girlfriend

Carolyn. Dan was there with his girlfriend Sandra. Tim was there with his girlfriend Lindsae. They grew up with Katy in Cleveland. She came with her son Jason. Jay likes one of Katy's nurses Jen. I know that he really likes her, because they were dancing most of the time. Especially when a slow song was playing. It was so much fun. Maria and Justin are really good dancers. They went to discotheques a lot. They would practice dancing at Tat's house before they would go out. Katy and Greg danced with everyone. They danced the Father and Daughter dance, and the Son and Mom dance too. I think Greg liked the Hokey Pokey dance the best. But there were other dances that everyone liked too. The chicken dance and the bunny hop are popular dances that everyone liked also. It was time for the bride to throw her bouquet. Dori caught it because she was pretty tall and strong. The garter toss was next. Greg took the garter off of Katy's leg with his teeth. The guys liked that and were cheering loudly. Casey caught the garter. Everyone was saying that it was fixed. By twelve midnight the city makes them shut down the hall. It's good for the dudes, because they were getting hammered. It was a great day for Greg and Katy, and all of their friends who danced up a storm. The bride and groom were getting ready to leave on their honeymoon when Tara, Young, Steve, and Ken were all saying their goodbyes. Is it the end of the supper club or just the beginning? I think it is a little of both. Greg and Katy were off to start their life together on their honeymoon in Hawaii. So it is back to ORD airport where this all began. They took a cab and Steve took back the Limo. I think beer can alley was Tara and his first stop. I bet Ken and Young were on their way there also. What will come in the future no one can tell, but with these nice people I think it will be great.

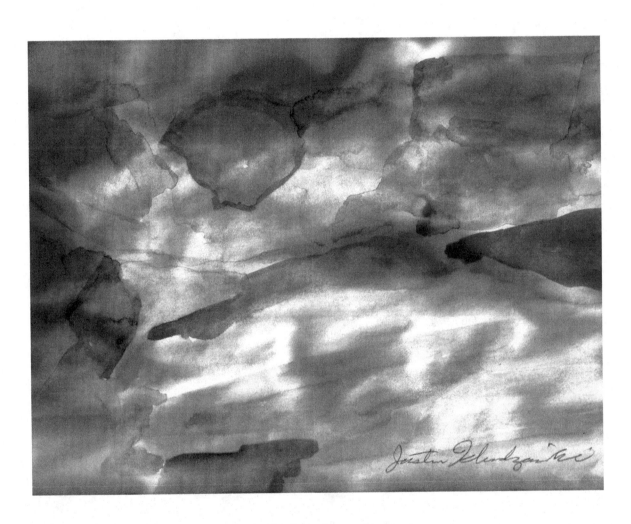

Islands in the stream

Reflections

Maria

I think of things the way they used to be
We dated and danced at the Rob Roy
I chased the train to get you to work
We got married and had fun
I was glad when I became a dad
We have been blessed with children like ours
I know it has been a rough ride
We made mistakes along the way
I have always hoped for our joy
We have to thank God for his help
I know that there is no good or bad
Only disagreements
We talked at night in bed of things to come
I love you just the same as I always have
By: Justin Thadd Kludzinski

Alfred

I remember you as a small boy
You wanted to play baseball with us big guys
I always liked you and your friend Marty
You two would crank call people
I think you wanted me to be your brother-in-law
You said I look like John the Beatle
I sold you my acoustic guitar
You always wanted to buy my 1977 Monza
I asked you to stand up for our wedding
You had grown so tall and full of life
I know Maria loved you very much
You had a great group called The Wayouts
I wish we could still hear you play
You got murdered that day
I lay with leukemia in my blood at Michael Reese
You will always be with us
I pray God brings you justice
It's been 20 years and your killers have not been found
At McDonalds of all places at 5:00 pm
Maria called me crying and said, "Alfred has been shot."
I asked, "Is he in stable condition?"
Maria said, "No he is dead."
I watched the news at night
I seen them take him away
We talked and felt I had let her down
I know my rage was an eye for an eye
What could I do?
I was just fighting to stay alive
She wrote to Unsolved Mysteries, and was on Ocurrio Asi
She changed her life, and turned to reading the bible
It did hurt us all in some untold ways
Alfred and Maria are now with our Lord
We look to the future
Our family is now so small
I see how it is to let grief rule us all
A glimmer of sun is bound to come
People don't give up hope is all that I ask
For Alfred was life even unto the last
Justin Thadd Kludzinski

Heart of Tata (Dad)

I know that he was not perfect
He got drunk and made my Mom cry
He felt bad the next day
Mom gave him the silent treatment
I would talk to him anyway
I knew there was something wrong
I felt it so strong
I think of his hardships
I wondered how he survived
I would be bitter
I would hold grudges
I know he loved people
I think that was his gift
I see the life in him flowing out
I learned to love my children the way he loved us
I had not told him that I love him enough
I learned to fish from him
He also taught me how to pick mushrooms
I watched baseball games with him
I played pinochle with him as his partner
I miss him so much
I don't know where his heart went
I hope that I have some of it
I know it was large
I think of all the people he helped in his life
I wonder what it takes to really see life
I think he showed me and I try to do right
I say a prayer for dear Tata tonight
Justin Thadd Kludzinski

Ma

You gave me life I am your first born
We are your four children Justin, Casey, Marie, and Cecilia
You gave us the love of a proud Polish American mother
You gave us guidance of Virgin Mary's Holy Way
The thing that I admired most about you is your lack of prejudices
Everyone was a human being none without a heart
The four grand kids all love you deeply that I know for sure
You were their dear Busi as they did call you so
Thaddeus, was your loyal loving husband
You have two Godchildren Margaret and Leon
I will first talk about Margie
As we the 12 other cousins did call her
My mother did play piano beautifully as I recall
She taught my cousin Margie to play a little song
It was "Your are my Sunshine my only Sunshine"
Leon she loved, and played monopoly with
Wanda my mother loved you also
You lived with us for awhile
I sometimes think of you as my third sister
Connie, Christine, Antoinette and Jerry
You also made her merry
Mark you became her good neighbor
Frank you're always very polite and had her dad's name
She had five brothers Thaddeus, Casimir, Henry, Conrad and Ray
I think Conrad was her favorite
He took her to Cubs games
She had one Sister Mildred who was older then Loretta
Three cool sister-in-laws Florence, Josie, and Francis
Then there was her Dad a businessman's dream
Busia her Mom, she had the best heart of the family
We will miss you so much
But I am sure there's a pinochle game
With all those good players
With the Father, Jesus, and the Holy Ghost
By: Justin Thadd Kludzinski

Dad

I long for your foot steps
I listen for your voice
I miss your touch
I even know your sound
I think of you often
I wait for my kiss
I talked with you until morning
I promise you this you always be missed
I remember the glimmer in your eyes now
I know you love Mom I seen it somehow
I have learn a lot now
I have you to thank
I have become better to people you see
I have you to thank there a friend you never seen
I know that a father is never that perfect
I see him his way but it is his heart that I long for until this day
By: Justin Thadd Kludzinski

Mikey

You were always there with a smile
A friend of my Mother and Dad
When I started working at Republic Steel
I came in high in pay as an electronics man
The others they shunned me because of it
They worked through the ranks
You were my glimmer of hope
We were friends from the start
You asked me, "Your Teddy's son?"
You introduced me to Richey
It all became good thanks to you I must say
The others they got to know me
Mikey thought I was okay
I seen you a lot at the show
When Marie and I would go
You never turned away
That was the true legacy of a friend all the way
Justin Thadd Kludzinski

To Jennifer

The leaves will change
The moon will shine
The wine will be fine in the summertime
I know you will be a star
You will not have to go far
Your heart is good
You know that you should
Write of love and heroes past
I know it can be a blast
From your Godfather Justin

Joan of Arc

Your white armor shined with God's light
He let you win the fight
St. Michael was at your side
St. Catharine help you cry
Never afraid of battle
Fire was your peril
You ask for the Pope at your trial
Bishop did so refuse because of his English bridle
You pray like Jesus in Gethsemane garden
They burn you with a guy dress as a red penguin
I know your fear death
As you took your last breath
God will never forsake you for heaven is yours
Because Jesus he open paradise doors
My heart is with you dear Joan
Love of us is set into stone
Justin Thadd Kludzinski

Ode ut Job (Ode to Job)

We all grump and gripe
We complain and snipe
We use God name in vane
We take the wrath of Cain
We know there will be trials
We use words to make our cuts
We see people for how they look
We know nothing from their book
We have suffered in this age
We should be like Job and break this cage
He endured all and stood by God
He did not forsake and this seemed odd
He lost his family and his wealth
He lost his love and this I felt
He was a believer all the same
He never let out any blame
I wish my ending comes with Jesus
I think of the heaven and that is a plus
I lost my Love and battled cancer
I know Our Father has an answer
I hope for wisdom from God's Holy Spirit
I can not wait for his final banquet
Justin Thadd Kludzinski

The Tower

I have been in the Tower
A clean sterile place
I knew that it was a very rough case
I pray for hope that the AML would erase
Then came the angels the nurses that you sent
It was like kissing my first girlfriend again
I will never forget how they cared for me
I know this for sure
The best people were with me
To give me new life
Their voices were soft and their eyes had a glow
Even that they did not know
The time I was with you rough as it was
My heart is my treasure you're all in there now
I'll never forget you so goodbye just for now
By: Justin Thadd Kludzinski

Alexis

You speak two languages what can they be?
Polish and English because you talk to me
Your brown eyes and hair communicate
The trust of a nurse that is out of sight
You're fun and have many friends
The work that you do can cause a lot of stress
I know you never leave anything a mess
Time you spend with friends will never end
So take a crossroad that splits your time
Have a drink with friends a margarita with lime
You treat people the way that you should
If only other people would
Every day you think about God
Justin Thadd Kludzinski

Erin

I know a great Polish nurse
It seems as if she walks 10,000 miles
She does good things for you and me
I see her smile on the run
She has too much work for just one
Listening is a thing that others don't do
But this girl has it on cruise control
She is a person of the world
I was glad to see
Forever brilliant like Venus's eye
I see wisdom in the sky
And she has both qualities which no one can deny
Justin Thadd Kludzinski

Gina

I know you caught me dancing to Poker Face
You ask how wife was doing with her cancer
You calm and steady with me
You offered to buy me Pizza when my eating was poor
I knew my welfare was in your thoughts
Your smile was always there
I felt safe in your care
That one of the reason I'm still here
It was great see the other day
I hope to see you when I return
May it be my last to Rush for AML
I hope that it never come back again
We will always be friends
Justin Thadd Kludzinski

Jen

This nurse has a heart of gold
Her blue eyes match the sky
Her hair is long and bold
Her demeanor glows like the planet Pluto
Tall and trim and very slim
She comforted me at fever's attack
Her skillfulness is very good
Let it not be misunderstood
She cares for people and her kindness shows
The clarity in her voice even though she talks softly everyone knows
She is needed wherever she goes
Justin Thadd Kludzinski

Maura

This nurse of mine always has the time
I needed her help when I had my fevers
She has a cool smile, and pretty blue eyes
Her Irish sense of humor comes through
She is a suburban girl, and a very
Likable person
She made the day to my introduction to
Chemo easier
I am glad to have her as my nurse
So let's all raise a glass in her name
To those who have gone far lest they
Not lose heart
Your work will be remembered by me

By Justin Thadd Kludzinski 5/30/11

Shama

A once in a lifetime Nurse with a sense of humor
Your black hair looks great and so do you
You come from Nepal which seems so far
But you bring hope like a shining star
Can you ride your bicycle with me some day?
In the city by the lake where the view is great
Your brother is your friend as I am too
You do good work and save me time
In time you will find your heart
What will be your choice may it be fulfilled
You should always talk and listen to friends and family
So love can make you grow the way you should

By Justin Thadd Kludzinski
May 29, 2011

Monica

I remember Jim Gibbons walk
The fun we had that day
My funny crazy dance with your son Jack
What cute little boy he remainders me of my son
At his age so full of life and innocent no hates
No prejudices just fun and love to all
I was really touched by him
It was my son
That helped me heal the first time
I think Jack played a hand this time
Jesus said it is through the mouth of babies
That we here Gods true word
You have a great husband Carl
Such a beautiful Daughter in Natalie
I really like your humor
The way you tease Lisa
As only an older sibling can do
I know because I am also a kidder
With the same tone
I also remember your kindness at walk
You gave me a ride to my car
Because of the long walk
You're Mom and Dad did such a good job
You have Dad sense of humor it so plain to see
I still remember the Christmas's gift
I bought a chair for Maria
We watched Dark Shadows together
Those were our last finally days
It was I know from your whole family
I think it was you as the tip of the spear
You get things done like your Father
I hope you like what I said
Stay nice and call me sometime
One day well drink some red wine
Justin Thadd Kludzinski

Lisa

I remember when your dad invited me over
We played ping pong into the night
It was nice with your Mom and Dad and Greg
It so sad not to have your Dad here
I also miss Greg his friend and mine
Your have a great sister Monica she is very nice
Your Mother is real a sweetheart
I know you're a teacher that is so kind
You try to open there minds
You have three beautiful children
Alex, David, and Amelia they all came to the SNIF
Alex and David like the Blackhawks
I like the pictures you show of them playing hockey
Amelia is next Marylou in Gymnasts
Casey has become such a good golfer
He is a great husband but you know
I know you got stuck looking for mushrooms
It is a Polish Childs curse
Theses forests we have are so bad
It just stickers and brush
Not like the Black forest of Germany
With its paths very grand
I would love to pick mudrooms there
My army friends taught I was crazy
I see my Dad and Yours laughing in heaven
I miss them just like you do also
Our world did get turned around
Love you and your great family
God must want me around
Give a kiss to your Mother
I love her Polish heart most of all
She always so nice to all the people she sees
Justin Thadd Kludzinski

74

Blue Eyes Look toward the Star

Christmas dawn is here
The son of man is near
Angels did appear
The shepherd's sheep did cry
You look into my eyes
And glance up at the sky
The star is there for all to see
Upon the hill sat wise men three
Mary and Joseph are happy the birth of Baby Jesus has come
We rejoice, for He is God's only son
By Justin Thadd Kludzinski

Aimee

We took a trip to QZ
You always held my arm
It brought me inner peace
I see your nice blonde hair flowing in the air
You have those beautiful eyes that sparkle like the stars
A journey we are on to find love in others arms
The future is the thing we can see it come
Some things you never say until its judgment day
I like the smile that is back
It's sad when it's away I tell you this today
Things that never change we always will remain
Dorothy and the Tin man will never be the same
I wish you everything from my heart you know
Always think of this my eternal kiss
Justin Thadd Kludzinski

Angel Knelt Beside Me

I was have another bad day
It was all I could do to keep death at bay
You sent me a angel Blonde and beautiful
With blue eyes that were never dull
She met my family and shows so much respect
My life had become a train disconnect
The pictures she has seen albums and poster boards set up there
Arranged by my sisters, daughter and nice could be functionaries
I knelt on right side of kneeler to say my good bye
I look to the left she knelt right beside me my angel so lovely
As said goodbye and touch my Mom's cold hands
She did the same and we were off to other lands
God is watching and he sends his best
We then had to lay my Mother to rest
By: Justin Thadd Kludzinski

Elisabeth

You are a lady from my father's country
You have eyes that are green and thoughtful
You have a heart as great as Chopin
You will be the reason the flowers will bloom
You shall always be a light to your daughter
You may help your son and his wife
You have three lovely grand children
You a your husband are blest by our God
You gave me prayers I needed with your sweet Aimee my friend
I glad you and her are my friends
Justin Thadd Kludzinski

Jessica (Lady Gaga)

You look as cute like in the Poker Face video
You were my bracket model at Gilda's Club
It then fits my daughter just right
I hope you meet her some day
It would be glad if would talk to my son
For he is so shy I wonder why
Because as you see I am a talkative guy
He is like Maria very quiet and holds his thoughts
Not like you and my daughter who talk a lot
I like your Mom she is cool
I almost thought we went to same high school
I want to say to your Dad he will be fine
It just takes a lot time
He will need your Love so much in days come
Have patience for he is the same
A Dad who loves his children well
Never let him get to down
Play Doctor Mario and Tetris Two
It helps to read the Psalms at times
Have him write his feeling down
I write poems are the way I found
But every one is unique so let him choose
Give him space
But do not leave him alone
It can be scary on your own
I was at home and I felt alone
With Maria, daughter, and son in the next room
They were walking on eggshells very much
I needed kisses and hugs to survey
So Love your dad all of time
Your humble friend Justin
Justin Thadd Kludzinski

Dennis

You hear drums of Krupa
That of Mick Fleetwood
You had a "Whole Lotta Love"
You have to ramble on
You know the stairway to heaven
You have a immigrates song
He digs deep dish pizza
He loves his steak tacos
He looks for his Vanishing point
He has golf's just for fun
He is in sales that is pressure
He like the Bears I'm sure
Good Fellows and Reservoir Dogs are his movies
He loves his dog as a buddy
He Loves Jessica his daughter
He loves Janet his wife
He is getting better
God will not let him down
It is the time to see life again
It is time to beat that drum
It is the time of the brave
I believe this because you are the one
I know the road back it is scary
I know it can not be fun
I know we all fight together
Take that cancer you bum
He will not scrum
Justin Thadd Kludzinski

The Ode to Jon

The love for Jansen was there
He was well aware
He was a Praetorian by all means
A hero for those who had not seen
He told you, his girlfriend to lay low
He protected her by guarding her so
He placed his body above hers
The shelter he gave saved her
His voice again will not be heard
If we could hear it for certain he would say
Come everyone and let us now pray
Jon was a man sent by God
The love he had in his heart we will always remember
By: Justin Thadd Kludzinski

The Ode to Tyrone Cab 202

This man is an unsung hero
He drives patients to their appointments
He listens to their hardships
He helps the son of a patient that dies
He bought me a hot dog after a ride
He talks about his hospital stay
He remembers a doctor a small Indian woman
He takes her advice and fights to survive
He talks about his friends and he gives them his soul
He is a good listener and tells you like it is
I think he is a brother in another life
May God Bless him the rest of his life
A friend who had cancer and shared a ride
By: Justin Thadd Kludzinski

Candy Girl

You see death first hand
You also see Hope
How do keep your smile
How do hide the tears
I always feel secure with you at my side
I know it hard to know us all
We come to you with recovery in sight
We are not sure all will survive
The touch of angel as you brush my neck
The heart of person that holds us so tight
A costume for Halloween along with us all
A cowgirl so cute and a hat nice and tall
Remember the words of baby you say to me
Remember the arms you hold how they need your help
Sweet girl we all grow to love you
God will always bless you my dear
Justin Thadd Kludzinski

Amy

I see many nurses because I get sick
But you are a very cool chick
Your blue eyes that greet people
Might knock them down on their seat
Mellow yellow is yours to behold
It is your smile that I find all wealth in
More than that which is in gold
You let me run to see all of my friends
Like they say the means justifies the ends
I wish you good things in my sly little way
Maybe we will get there with my trusty sleigh
Thank you for being there for me in my recent stay
This boy is on the loose and now it's time to play
I think you're a lot of fun
But I have got to run
The horse is at the gate
Maybe someday it will be a date
Justin Thadd Kludzinski

Chrissy

I talk a lot of the way I learn to dance
How you always have to take a chance
I also told you of stereo love and poker face
That BMT might have to get some mace
This dancing patient chemo and all
It something I carried into the hall
You like to dance you have said
You like grape jelly on your bread
The blue eyes you have now make four
It must be a prerequisite for the 9 floor
I think you would look great in a hiked up green skirt
I know I can find a classy green shirt
We could dance it fast and we could dance it slow
If you're married or engaged that would be such a blow
It was fun to talk with you as cool as the snow
I wonder do really have a beau
It is like I promise so nurse beware
Love is not kind and seldom is fair
Justin Thadd Kludzinski

Jenny 9

You are a spark plug
You never swept underneath the rug
You like Blue I have been told
It so great when you're not IV Poled
I think of water and your eyes of blue
Your kind and gentile like Winnie the Pooh
I hope you do not like honey
It better if you are like bunny
As cute as you are
I would see you in a cool car
I thought you were one swinging fun nurse
I bet you have a cool purse
Thanks for the care and the smile
I think you have such cool style
Remember me as you go
Justin the crazy old schmo
Justin Thadd Kludzinski

Kimberly

You have been so nice
We have met more than twice
You swabbed mine nose
For what I do not know
You listen to me read
Of this I can succeed
You fixed up my thumb
I hurt it being so dumb
You got my parking pass
Now I can push on the gas
You ask me if I ate
But I was running late
You are great to me
Friends will always be
Justin Thadd Kludzinski

Laura

You been at Rush 13 years
You have seen many of tears
You like a blouse in hunter green
You have always been so keen
You let me go to 11 to see my friends
You always buck the trends
You hate dictators like I do
I said Nero was probably number two
You think Adolph was the worst
Stalin had such an evil thirst
I think God will punish them
It like removing some phlegm
It was a blast talking with you
I am glad you are part of the crew
So be cool and stay as fresh on all topics
I hope to see you some day at the flicks
Justin Thadd Kludzinski

Aaron

I knew your Dad, Mom and Lisa
Brian is a great army friend
Peg was a very great host
Lisa was cute as a button
I know you were in country
It had to have been hard
Things that stay with you always
The friends and brothers in arms
I met you only once when Matt and I went to the hall
To see the fire of Brian and kindness of Peg
You want to run for president
I tried this once myself
Got the form from New Hampshire
They want $1,000.00 it's more than
Maria would let me spend
You have a nice wife and two children
You know that the money is not there
We used to talk about this a lot
Brian, Howard and I
If we were President
I know you have strong opinions
The second amendment is one
I believe strong in this one
My brother-in-law Alfred was murdered
in this town
With hard laws around
We have the most murders, so who got it wrong
I'm glad to have met Lisa on the way to Arizona
I'm glad she is doing so well
You take care now Aaron the family comes first
Remember November 11 we are brothers
In arms
So go pick up Brian and eat dinner
I like Applebee's they treat veterans the best
By: Justin Thadd Kludzinski

You are a Child

I remember the baby sitting in the car seat
Who grew up to be so sweet
She is strong and that's not hollow
Leaves turned red she did not follow
I seen her once when the train did come
At I time when I was young
We ate pizza and had some fun
Matt's so happy you were the sun
You grew up well that I know
I just thought that you should be told
Your family loves you their hearts bestowed
So let's all see the morning when it comes
So we can see your face you are the sun
By: Justin Thadd Kludzinski

Peg

I remember when I first met you
I was at the EM club with Hank
I knew Brian at work he told me you were his wife
I ask Brian if it was okay to ask you to dance
I did like are fast dance a twist I do think
I did like your good friendship we play Pinochle a lot
I like the ski trips to Garmisch and Berchtesgaden
I remember the Linder Hoff trip and French wine we had
I though it was such a nice gesture to have
Howard and I for Thanksgiving
I can see Lisa in her car seat
I drove in the cool red car that you and Brian had
I tried your squash it was best
I was invite for chicken that was made so good
I record The Carpenters all on one tape
I got your letters at Christmas time
I visited with Matthew while at the hall
I met your son Aaron and knew Lisa from before
I tried to be happy like you and Brian are
Justin Thadd Kludzinski

Brian

I met you in Augsburg in the ASA
You were the best Controller on our shift
We work together to get all machines up
We became friends through Hank and Chuck
You invited us to dinner many a time
Hank and I were partners in the Pinochle we played
You and Peg were partners
But I had to learn to play double deck
We had some great games
I remember you work with leather and made me a blue belt
You also dye my baseball glove all blue so I could play
I had three color glove red, white and blue
But it was against the rules so you helped me out
You also learn piano and were great at skiing
We took a lot trips to see Linder Hof castle and Oktoberfest
You drove me to Munich to get my trip on leave to London
We pull CQ together and let all he girls inside
When Chuck was going back
We drank 14 bottles of white wine German of course
I remember the Guest houses we drank some Gespritzter
We always had a blast
You are very good friend is was fun to visit you with Matt
I hope your book is almost done I like the work you have done
So from the guy name Ski I hope you still have fun
Justin Thadd Kludzinski

Howard

Your middle name is Winston
I think it rather swell to be name after a famous leader
You are a chess master I only one game against you
We were clever bunch techs
The lifers had no chance
We bought an old rug from housing surplus
I had a big rust stain but we knew what to do
The purple Ritz dye it covers it so well
A Bissell rug sweeper we got
It saves us so much time no buffing floors today
Some dusting here a there the EM Club was calling our names
They bugged just the same but we were home free
Top sergeant was a lifer and the Captain was West Point
I beat him in the football pole by one point
He said I should not give you your pay
But I could tell he was impressed
These crazy hippies' guys dress in this army stuff
I know you; Joe had it down as 31S20
We were the Pros from Dover with Charley, T and JR
There was no shift that could touch us
That is the power we all had
I glad we took the trips to castles and towns
The pass in Innsbruck in the winter time
Your Ramble did the job there but it was pretty rough
Frankfurt and pizza with the fried egg and Jalapeno
Norte Dame 24 and Alabama 23 best college game ever
The fireworks in the street rockets' one corner verses another
The time you went in a glider over Augsburg
The trip with your Mom and Dad to Rome
You met Pope Pal VI and told me the pizza sucked
We had some very cool times
So as a line cutter I say have a very good day
Justin Thadd Kludzinski

Charlie

You reported to Augsburg as a new guy
I remember you were not ever shy
You quickly became friends with us line-cutters
Your machines were glad you got there you got them to purr
You and I play on the company volleyball team
I think your serve was a laser beam
You had to roommates of JR and Joe with all his smoke
I think Joe made you and JR choke
You and I went Neuschwanstein
And climb the mountain on the right
I think it was the coolest thing we ever did do
You had your VW Beetle and we would drive to work
I knew this one MP was always such jerk
You came to my house for our wedding
It was in May in the spring
You seen my lawn chair front room furniture
I got a couch twice sent then with all three cats' fur
You made a great impression with Maria and all my friends
I think you will always be there in the end
Justin Thadd Kludzinski

JR

You came to Augsburg a Rookie
You found the phony underground shop
You became a junior ground hog
You got your name on that plot
You always wanted to see snow
You ran outside the first time it came
You were put with the rough house gang
You got the mighty Joe and cleaver Charley
You were the new guy so dues had to be paid
You then became my new roommate
You and I got along well we like the same music
You told me about Jonnie Mitchell I went bought Court and Spark
We darn near wore that 8 track out
You told me of your girlfriend Peggy back in Tampa
You talk of your wedding to come when your tour was done
You became a great Crypto Tech like the rest us bums
You were our best short centerfielder but not
the couches son (manager's buddy)
You were always a line cutter but not a worm head (Jody) like some
You and I would always have a catch like brothers have done
You have your girl and children well done
You are my friend a old ASA one
You take good care and on Veteran's day drink
a toast to northwest for friend that
You knew way back in the day
Vigilant Always I say
Justin Thadd Kludzinski

Castles

The world has many great Castles
I have seen but a few
The rest I leave up to you
I have a quest to see them again
The group I am in we see many of them
Linda is dreaming of the rooms as they lay
Mona is talking of being a Queen and dungeons and stuff
Gary is telling us were we might go to find theses gems
I talk of defense my Army side shows
We have many people who love them all the same
I hope not to forget someone's name
I think of day when we four can go
To the best castles ever and drink some good wine
I hope we meet people there
Who ever becomes our friend
The flag that we fly is worth more to us
We are the new Knights and Princesses of this age
By: Justin Thadd Kludzinski

Mona

You came to know me through Castles
First you were another good Princess
Then you became a torturer Queen
You want to be wicked the Jutes were your prey
Your cousin was not detecting this
When Gary and I arrived
I seen your heart changing
You became the person I know today
The love is in you quotes of your words
You care with a silent voice
The vision of your trip runs through our heads
You have shown me some kindness
I dare say it is so for some turmoil has found me
You have been a the relief that I need
A Knight of the darkness I look for the light
I see hope in you for love is your code
Remain my dear friend till the end
By: Justin Thadd Kludzinski

Dear Mary

I do not know you
I do but love you
I do but tell you
I have just been you
I can only say that you have a friend
I do this for Mona my friend
I know she helps in the end
I called her the queen of hearts
I know she helps mend hearts
I know it strange and unreal
I know pain is a pill
I take it on quite days
I know God is your help
I found some peace in the psalms
I think you want to hide
I say be right at Mona's side
I no days will go bye
I try not to cry
I know sadness will come
I know you need some fun
I think of the future I wonder
I know there more to come
I want you happy again
I want you to face the sun
I want heart to find love
I want book 2 to begin
I speaking from sorrow
I speaking for a tomorrow
Justin Thadd Kludzinski

The Knight of England (Gary)

The color red is your color
Is the braveness of your blood you had to shed
The country has seen you serve
May we all have been so brave
The Queen and our Princess have been in our charge
We love them and protect them the best we know how
The gifts that you have given to those my seems small
I tell you this it is big and has greatness
The best is most of all the friendship of us four friends
I know for myself it has been so much fun
Together we travel with sword and with shield
I know that Mona and Linda are right by our side
I dedicate this to you my great Facebook friend
Let the wine of happiness be always at you side
By: JustinThadd Kludzinski

Linda

The one of the good Princesses of my story
You dream of great castles
The were the interior is gold and diamonds are many
You wait for prince charming a handsome soul
He is on his way to find you some day
The cousin of yours from north has become Queen
You have met Gary and Justin for they have come here to help
The love of all castles Gary has shown us so many
You wonder and ponder the next one we will see
For we must see them all so wee can be free
The grottos, the dining rooms, the towers
The lawns, the flowers, the moats, and the mountains
I know you will find the prince that you seek
I hope he is good and heart made of gold
A future with a good person is best to be remember
The rest is with God for he knows the best
By: JustinThadd Kludzinski

Queen Mother

I now a Queen of South
She is sad today
I like her a lot
May this help she lost her Queen Mother yesterday
We all love Linda so it is with heavy heart I say
God will send her to protect you and your family as an angel
So may say for Mona, Gary, Gene, Rachelyn, Robert, Siham, Betty and I
Bless you darling and we wish you are support
Think good fun things you did with her
Remember stupid arguments and how small they seam now
Just to have her say hey my little daughter how are you now
Prayers and good wishes from my heart
I know my Mom and Wife just die
You want to cry but stay strong others need you
But if you do cry make it for a good time not a bad
Her life has more meaning that way
For in darkness there shall be light
In hopelessness there will be hope
Sorrow brings forth joy
Pity turns to strength
Despair is replaced by memories of her life
Our mind is his infinity of our soul
Love is the constant
Justin Thadd Kludzinski

Veronica

On this Halloween you should be seen
Some girls are always mean
You have long hair like your Mom
I know you went to your prom
People know God went they need him
You have never forsaken him
Hard work is the way to salvation
You know good works can give deliberation
The time is not know for us all
We are souls who travel the malls
Remember what you learn as a child
Innocent and full of zest
Your Mom is always the best
I leave a thought for reflection
Love with your heart not your mind
You think better in time
Justin Thadd Kludzinski

Justin the Blue Knight of Wales

We see this man old and sick
I see him young and well
We can not believe his words
I can but say all is true
We think he pass his prime
I do not share this view
We think his dreams are not real
I think it possible if God does too
We know he talks of fun in the sun
I know he looks for love when the moon comes
We talk of his heart his failures to know
I do not expected others to know
The heart is a place we all must go
BY Justin Thadd Kludzinski

Siham

You are the new girl and brought us the
Green of Ireland and towers in Spain
You are a very cute girl
Your dimple is cool
Your hair is jet black that lights up your face
You seem to have fun and must love the sun
I think you will join are four castles troupe
For as the Blue knight of Wales I offer my lance
Your ribbon I will put there along with my two Queens
The green one is yours with
Mona's Light Blue and Linda's Gold
And Gary is to be are King of this I was told
Are table is round like Arthur's was once
We meet by lake of lady unknown In Inverness
Were we start are quest of four strangers back then
The castles are there so let us share join us my lady
Come today as moonlight does come
Tomorrow look east for we shall begin
By: Justin Thadd Kludzinski

Robert the White Knight of Augsburg

He is a gallant lad
He fights for right
He takes in beauty as a site
He talks with goodness
He lives for adventure
He helps the poor in every town
He works for God and God alone
He follows rivers to the seas
He loves the gardens as the come
He is a good sport in Knightly games
He likes his Queens and Princess to
He rides with King Gary and Justin Blue
He guards the fair Ladies with Gene the Green
He is for Justice in every land
He speaks of Quest that God has told
He looks for a certain cup of gold
By: Justin Thadd Kludzinski

Distant Drum

Off in distance a drum is heard
It is a friend so far away
She has the look of mysterious beautiful girl
The tides are calling that keep us away
Moon let the tides bring her my way
An ancient ocean of Greek times
A blue Sea flows near her home
Will we storm castles with the rest of our group
I see a aura of coincides of old
A reincarnate of lovers past
As winds go west and to east they blow
The wine of life is to go on
Shadows have showed us it can be bad
Hope comes from faith in God
Will the future be bright
Is thief coming for me tonight
No one knows the answers
Beating of my heart carries me now
Justin Thadd Kludzinski

Rachelyn

I know you are one that comes here for fun
We have got yours hugs nice as they come
The castles you share have been great to us all
I have seen through your heart
A nice gentle one
A shy girl you are and talk so refine
Come dance at our Ball that Linda put on
I promise you that
For then the suitors so many will come
You be with next to Mona she will tell you a tale
Gary will find you and he will get a dance
Gene will but make you laugh and rejoice
Siham will tell you of mystery old
I know little about you if I am so bold
The happiness is there for you to be told
We all welcome your very good soul
By: JustinThadd Kludzinski

Gene the Green Knight of Ireland

We know he likes a joke
He gives Linda advice
We seen his reaction
He has a dry humor
We all like it very much
He guards our Queens
We gave him Sir Robert
He ask us for more
We said hold your horses
He never makes his bed
We said Linda will teach him
He looks for the bubble bath
We told him see Queen Linda
He talks of some termites
We know it was some French Knights
He will come back tomorrow
We know he from Ishpeming Michigan
He has a new Cobra
We know he will drive it
He is a great member and has arrived
By Justin Thadd Kludzinski

Ulli

The girl from Konigsberg we welcome you
We see from your photos you share with us all
I live in your country for two years
The castles you have are great to be seen
I have love my trip up and down the Rhine
King Ludwig was crazy or that what they say
I love his three castles the grotto is great
Munich has Oktoberfest the beer is so good
My home town was Augsburg a city of fun
The café was great, has you have coffee and strudel
I dance at the Teeny Bar to fly robin fly
The German white wine was Liebfraumilch
I know you bring us a lot good things
So deep from my heart Gruss Gott my Fraulein
By: JustinThadd Kludzinski

Babe

I remember what you told me
She did not feel the same
I could tell she was important
She stayed right by your side
I think a dog can do this to say she is alright
She always wants to please you each and every day
I think you like her kisses as sloppy as they are
She always there to protect you
I know what a good pet can be
She give you love so greatly
I could never match
She is the one to count on
I wish she would let be your closest friend
She always be the first one I know reason why
I asking things for myself
She would think of only you
I leave you now and her but love me just the same
Justin Thadd Kludzinski

Bob

When you're a spy in trouble
Who do call Bond, James Bond 007
When you're in Dialysis Unit with the water coming in
Who you going to call Bond, Bob Bond
The light is going bad and the ballast are all screw up
He is the man to call
The thing that makes him great
He believes in God and treats the people fair
I like him as a friend and person too
He has a Son name Nick he very proud of him
And the things he has done in College
As junior it is very grand to make your own app
He is like his father's son he has learn from the master Bob
The apprenticeship has begun
He has taught him many things
He brought him with him to fix our chairs upholstery he did learn
The thing I like with Bob he always has the time
To help solve a problem even at your home
The knowledge and skill is something you must have
Bob is at the Top so let's give the man a cheer
I would be remise not say it so
Goodness he will always show
Justin Thadd Kludzinski

Mike

We play catch at one day at old Scottsdale
I found out you were lefty handed
I never caught a lefty it seem weird at first
I keep reach across like would a righty
I guess there is always a first
We became friends at get go
You like Cubs just like me
We have a friend in who a Dietarian
We think see is just the most
I think have to say she is a Betty
I think this you concur
The thing that did while a lay there
3 years ago it might be
The Connie's Pizza did sustain me
It lasted for 4 whole days
When everything tasted like metal
The Chemo has a strange way it does
But you came to my rescue
Brought some food I could eat
You said prayer that helps my spirit
God send you as angel Gabriel
He knows what he doing and how
So my friend till our next lunch
Or a party sometime your stay a true friend of mine
Justin Thadd Kludzinski

Artist Judy

You battle hot and humid summer
You paint with grace like Picasso
You like your boots both black and brown
You never have any snow to push around
You took good care of children
You send them back to school again
You have lot paintings there
You have them up and down the stairs
You are a person that really cares
You are my friend like my beloved Bears
You have the Dolphins and the fish
You must cook Marlin for a dish
Justin Thadd Kludzinski

The Olde to Doctor Veronica

You came to me as I found her
I will always remember that day
You know I needed your help then
I know Cher sang "turn back time"
You were the bridge that could help me
I seen her take her last breath
You know how much I love her
I had tell my children she was no longer not easy thing to do
You have brought me so far now from the ides of March
I know book two has already been open
You have lighten my heart
I have a challenge ahead of me
You found me the way
I am sad that your leaving we all have to walk on are own someday
You gave me the courage to go on dear
I am glad Dr. Elizabeth Rich sent me to you
You are a Latina like Maria and that made it easy to talk to you
I think God made the connection before we met on that day
You will always have a place doctor somewhere deep in my soul
I will never forget the kindness you show
You can always say I knew a writer name Justin he fought for love
I say I knew a Doctor names Veronica she made me have hope
By: Justin Thadd Kludzinski

Colin

You have survived Cancer
You work very hard for the
Leukemia Research Foundation
You played in band and have fun
You work on Jim Gibbon's Race in June
You have good Judy she helps so much
You gave me support to beat this thing
You are good friends and hear our stories
You get the sponsors we all need
You get the help from ABC
You set the course in Lincoln Park
You know were we been
You're the best
I wish you continued success
Justin Thadd Kludzinski

Beloved

We are in a time of uncertainty
I wonder when the thief in the night will come
We see him as Lucifer
I know that Michael shall beat him again
We must guard our souls
Temptation is everywhere
We must look to the Holy Spirit for answers, for wisdom
I hear sad hearts
We all need love
I know Jesus can bring it to us
We good people of God the Father gather together
I see Virgin Mary weeping
We need to be like saints
I know that it is hard to have faith
We have to have faith and hope
I know that charity helps
We must dance with the Lord
He gives us solace
We forget him too much
When things are good, He is last in our thoughts
We call to Him in bad times
God will never desert us because He loves us
Let's put our trust in Him
Justin Thadd Kludzinski

Romeo and Juliet

Has dawn found us alive my Juliet
It has my Romeo
What are we to do my dearest
I do not know the world does hate us
No my love it hates our love
It might be so
For families seldom know love
Yes honor and reputation not of hearts
Romeo my lover we kiss and world stops
Juliet has not the moon shone in your eyes
For souls tremble as we walk in innocents
As my passions longs for you
But what of our parents will they not see
Alas my being rest with thee
And I nothing without you my love
Justin Thadd Kludzinski

Elegy of a Walk

We walk with open minds
It flows like a river in our thoughts
To center of our problems
Life is cruel and harsh at times
The solitude is refreshing
What has been and what will be
Feet do ache and blisters come
I sometimes like to run
Your pulse is rapid at least 110
Part of me would wish it would end
Just like the planes of Marathon in ancient Greece
The running of the first was by Pheidippides
He ran 26.22 miles twice and then he said
We have conquered
He then did collapse and die
Would this be my last Goodbye
Justin Thadd Kludzinski

Elegy of Disappointments

I feel that life sometimes is a disappointment
It can happen oh so fast
From happy to sad in less than a hour
The euphoric fire can be quenched
As with all are emotions we must rebalance
Less we succumb to the path of unhappiness
Love does provide the healing needed
Its face can be two fold
Expectation from it might hurt if taken wrong
Those of a friend and that of a lover
A quandary becomes to know what to do
We all have fond this choice at one time in our romances
What can be a that tell tale rule
I know it is outwardly hard to take that last step
Mankind would wither if we did no take it
Kisses tell the heart how it will end
Justin Thadd Kludzinski

Elegy of Resurrection Mary

It was Halloween 1976 Disco was stile alive
The Rob Roy Disco was not even a Dive
My Brother and I were looking for chicks
The Commodores were building with bricks
I seen a hot blonde and ask her to dance
Boz Scaggs was playing so I took a chance
It was Lowdown followed by Harbor Lights
Here blue eyes just so way out sights
As we pulled in close for the slow song
I asker was she from Hong Kong
She said no I am Polish like you
I guess then you must be Sue
She said I am Mary how about you
My names Justin and I very much like blue
We kissed after the dance
I think I was in a trance
Mary comes this way to my table it is here
I would like offer you some cheer
There is my Brother Casey over there
Mary disappeared in thin air
Casey knows that I wasn't that drunk
I bet you think I am some kind of a Punk
Then we here'd the ghost stories on the WIND
We just thought for a moment what
And just grinned
By: Justin Thadd Kludzinski

America Were Are You Now

The grace that God did give you
It is be cause faith that you have been so great
You must come back to God of that there is no mistake
Our love of every people is that of God's own light
Freedom is are birth rite and help us keep are might
I share on Independence Day with freedom at my side
The sacrifice of many who fought to keep us free
We are a nation of souls who stand up all together
We dream of life worth living
So let's bring back the hope
A militia I will make of patriotic people
That brings God back up to the plate
This November we must not wait
By: Specialist Fifth Class Justin Thadd Kludzinski

Graduate

The time to look forward is now
But remember to take from the past
The wisdom of the old
Stay true with your heart
It can help you when you need it most
Remember God and always pray
Trust friends that are good and just
Try not to make a fuss
Have fun and enjoy the rush
Play sports and dance and sing
There is time to get the rings
Start a family and other things
You work so hard in school it seems
Take a breath its good fresh air
I believe in you so world beware
Goodness is coming with you there
By: Justin Thadd Kludzinski

CVS

As high school goes it is the best
It taught me so much
Aviation, power plant and air frame
Electronics and electricity
Drafting and Machine shop
Foundry and R.O.T.C.
English and literature
Algebra and geometry
Shakespeare and mythology
Physics and History
Drinking and smoking, was not the best think this I know
Riots and friends of all races
Football and 16" softball
Fighting and fireworks
Dick Butkus and Moose Cholak in the same division no less
My good friend PFC Dennis (Buster) Eugene Wisniewski
Who died in Vietnam on 3/1/1969 born on 2/12/1948
Saved men as a Medic, because he was a conscientious objector one day
Then he stepped on a land mine in a supposed cleared area two days later
He was the captain of my newspaper agency
I took over after he went in the Army
What a good dude he was
He taught me how to be a paper boy
So our great school builds our character like none other
Forever a CVS Cavalier till I die
Justin Thadd Kludzinski

Happy Thanksgiving

I am always happy that I met you.
The first day was at the House of Hughes
You never gave me the blues
I wish we could go back there
I miss seeing your face
The eyes that set the sky to the same color
The heart that gave like none before
The listening to me in my sorrow
You told me to hold on for tomorrow
I thank God for helping me get to know you
The angel of the morning
I must say adieu may love find you
Happy Thanksgiving Always Justin

Max the Cat in my Hat

I remember him as a nice and gentle cat
Who was afraid of Matthew's yellow coat
He hated the noise that plastic bags would make
It would make him jump
He would wait for Matt like a dog, until he came home from work
He would sit next to me on the chair's arm rest
I would pet his head until he fell asleep
If I stopped petting his head, he would give me his paw
That was his way of letting me know to continue my work
He liked to sunbathe whenever he saw a patch
of sun appear anywhere in the house
He ate grass outside, when he would escape
He came back when Matt would call his name
Without him it will never be the same
We all love you and miss you what a shame
The thoughts we have of you will always remain
Justin Thadd Kludzinski

Pixie

I wonder how you cope
With the loss of your owner Maria
She was your world
You guard her sewing room
Her sacred shrine
Let no one enter on this Thanksgiving Day
When Martha tried you chased her away
In that room we had a rocker
We used it as a baby's room then
We rocked our Jessica and Matthew
To my father's Polish baby song
Aaa Kotki Dwa
Pixie likes to sleep on the big orange cushion
In the rocker that Maria bought her
I see she comes by me now
We are now just us three
You lay in my lap and steal heat
You scratch if I try to move
I think you don't want to let me go
You're scared I will not come back
You let me pet you now, not like before
That is quite a trick
Maria was the only one who could do this
I know we miss her but have no fear
I am with you now
Justin Thadd Kludzinski

Wild Horses

Wild horses I will ride them some day
I do this for two friends
One day we will ride in the sunset
We stopped by the brook and listened for sounds
I talked about my loves both lost and just found
We will gallop as long as the horses want to
I spotted your eyes, and they looked the same as they did before
We stopped riding and sat down
You laid your head on my lap
I brushed your hair, and kissed you very slowly
The horses began to neigh as if saying it is time to go
I had such a beautiful day being with you
We must ride again, Sir Nugget cannot wait
I love you for your gracious heart
We must find the time off from work yet to visit again
I know it was a sudden ride to the west
For now we must depart, but we will meet again
Keep all of your courage and don't lose your heart
Your cowboy is coming back
Some sunrise he will just appear
By: Justin Thadd Kludzinski

The Quality of Mercy is not Strained

I think of war
I think of peace
I think of the dead
I think of life
I think of hate
I think of love
I think of revenge
I think of forgiveness
I think it's time to think of both
I think it's time to stop it all
I think God wants us to share the love
I wish I could have a hand in there
I feel that He gives me this chance
I know that I have the heart to do it
I'm not sure my mind is that clear
I have the faith and that will tell
I hope I do not go to hell
I want to be with the Lord our God
I know that the Son above is love
And God the Father has the final say
Wisdom is the Holy Spirit
I do not know the hour of my demise
I only hope my love survives
I want those to love me for whom I am
I am just a humble man
Justin Thadd Kludzinski

Cancer

What ugly word
It means death to me
Hurts all people young and old
Brave and bold
Small and Large
Quite and loud
Rich and poor
It is the love of nurses that helps you along
The kindness of the PCT's that makes the morning bright
Food servers and janitors
That break up your day telling a joke along the way
Doctors and teams study you so well
Will I find heaven or will it be hell
At night my mind wanders
It is so hard to process
Why did it come to me
The night sweats hit me
My bed is like a lake
Will my suffering abate
In comes my wife her side is in pain
I said what is wrong she is not sure
I go home it still bothers her
Go get checked out Maria my dear

Wouldn't you know it is cancer too
They work with us together when I get chemo she does not
She gets Chemo I do not
It hard to be patient and caregiver all in one year
She did all the right things and radiation also
But Uterine Cancer came back at stage 4 on her liver and lungs
The gave her less than a year
Then came the ides of March
She took her last breath
I held her hand as Cher sang "Turn back Time"
I call for the nurse and doctor, they both rushed in
They said she is gone
I felt a sad tear as I walk
To tell my daughter and son
Also my sister her best friend
My cousins were there too in the cafeteria visiting at that time
I came on Sunday March 3 2013
Why was it her and not me
It seams quite unfair she was so young
But Cancer doesn't care
Justin Thadd Kludzinski

Desire

Sometimes we want things
It seems out of reach
A pretty girl
The fast car
Dream home
Family a boy and girl
But are these the things we covet
I say no it is health
It is peace
God must be there also
But love is the answer
With it those other things do matter
Without not much happiness
For on today tell your Valentine of your love
Hold her heart kiss her long
May the rest be done in passion
Till the next blazing dawn
Justin Thadd Kludzinski

Cold

What is it to us
It comes as arctic storm
Weathermen smile as it comes
Talk of records and such
To homeless it means death
A frozen uncaring tragedy
If we all could help them some how
Not by the nickels and dimes
But by love that is not there
Why did they come to this fate
Dreams that have fallen so low
Cars my not start when it's below
Is that worst than there plight
Do the rest of look the other way
Look deep into your souls
Are you that someone so cold
Justin Thadd Kludzinski

Wrigley Field

The world has many great Baseball Parks
I know that this is the Best
The Need to fix it like the rest
I support the Cubs in their Plans
The group has many new plans
The Hotel and ramp are important to guest who will come
The Video boards in left and in right are aright
The Bathrooms are still way too small so let them fix them
An elevator for those who might need one
Parking the neighbors will love you make as much as you need
The food we want all the best vendors to show Chicago Pride
I hope not keep my Beloved Cubs in the Dark Ages
The plans are needed so pass them and have a nice day
For my Uncles, Ron, Jack and Harry do not stand in the way
I hope we meet you good people in the new Wrigley one day
Game Seven of our World Series win
We are all Chicago so let us be fair
Justin Thadd Kludzinski

Be my Valentine

I am the big heart of a Delphinium
You have the enthusiasm of Bouvardia
I love you and your refined beauty
Like that of the purple orchid
You and red tulips are the perfect love
I wish for us to be like
Stock butter yellow that of lasting love
You are like a lavender rose full of enchantment
I think the most of you dear
Will we ever draw near?
So hearts can find a way
Be my Valentine today
Justin Thadd Kludzinski

Breakfast at Tiffany's

I know this was classy
I think of Audrey she was the best
I remember her legs
I can still see her eyes
I would believe she smelled like flowers
I slow kiss her on the lips
I listen to her talk for hours
I know that she was full of love
I see her smile that is forever
I felt her heart as it is beating
I recognized her laugh when she came
I found her cat in an alley
I saw her cry because I had brought him
I remove the hat from her head
I hug and kisses her has taxi roar off
I guess you can say that I like it
I wish I was there that day
By: Justin Thadd Kludzinski

Ode to the last Unicorn

It was a long time ago in ancient Jutland
In the fogs of the fjords
Stands the white horned horse of old the last unicorn
He runs from hunters his heart to burst
His family is gone
They close in on him
He jumps on and floats on a big piece of ice
He makes it to safety and into a hidden cave
On February 29 he is seen sometimes
In parts of the world to find a mate
We want him safe God
Help him find a new wife to bring more unicorns
Into the world to live a new life
The rich and the poor have hunted him
When will his journey find its happy end?
So dream big and look to the north
His time is coming wait for him

Justin Thadd Kludzinski

Angelina

I know you are scared
Cancer is an ugly word
I have beaten it three times myself
I just lost my wife of 32 years
It was Uterine Cancer in March of 2013
I tell you this to help with your problems
For God must be in your Picture
He was in mine the Psalms were the most comforting
I know your family means the most to you
You would not have done what you went through
I think you will be Lara Croft and break the tomb
That has taken so many
I love for your heart and courage
I believe you will see your Grandchildren
I tell you from my experience do not get half empty
Stay always half full
I have a friend who does that for me
It does not always have to be family member
A person to talk to on any level
My nurses and co workers cheer me up the most
The family has too much gloom in their eyes
Music is great I was caught dancing to Poker face
The nurses laughed do not forget to laugh
Do not cry just say hi
A little girl came up to me in church
She gave me a the sign of peace
It brought me back to life
It is the little everyday things that matter
My son said Dad when you coming home it was light
From God he was only four years old at the time
I pray for you and you're Family
Please get well we all love you
Justin Thadd Kludzinski

Ashley

I knew you knew I would do this
The cool vampire named Alice
I like your sweet smile
The others in your house really dig you
I can see that for sure
The fame has not gotten you
I listen to you on your Facebook
The people complement you for always for being so very real
I think you will be a star in my movie
The plot is still very thin
I know that you are very respectful
The family of yours is all very proud
I am glad you're my friend
The guys must think you are fun
I wish I was young
The way opens the future is clear
I see an academy award is near
The night is has come but watch out for the sun
By: Justin Thadd Kludzinski

Ben

The Boston Red Sox are your middle name
You save the day in Pearl Harbor
Daredevil did find his Elektra
The Iranians thought you were Canadian
In town the folks thought you were a bank robber
A Dark Knight is on your horizon
You have a friend name Matt
Your Son and Daughter who love you
Jennifer is a glowing beauty you're such a lucky guy
Good will is always worth hunting
You help stop Armageddon
Alanis found you in Dogma
Our fears were adding up
Did we ever find Amy
You did not let Rudolph play
Oscar seems to have found you
The Emmy seem light years away
Drive but stay in your lane
Shakespeare was always in love
By: Justin Thadd Kludzinski

Bill

It is in the hole
That's the facts Jack
You had love that was lost in translation
Had daughter who scissors a kid
Was a friend named Bob
You were the one they called
But Mona back in the Louvre in Paris
Live the same day with a beautiful lady
The royal T's was a Raleigh Saint
Saturday night was always fun
Charlie let you watch his angels
Rushmore was MR. Blume
You did some bowling now and again
Will our Cubs ever win
Justin Thadd Kludzinski

Brooklyn

You were stalked at airport
But now the ball is in Andy court
North Carolina is long and far away
In Austin I would rather play in clay
Family just has to bring their dogs
I believe Texas has some frogs
A blonde beauty you must surely be
I am sure William and Kate will have you for tea
Serve is term that you might know
I just watch you on the Tonight Show
Do not let Bob and Billie roam
I bet you even have a nome
You have been illustrated in smallest of swim suits
Secrets was also had its hoots
I am glad you got your wings
Your beauty has know hidden strings
I say Merry Christmas my dear
May it be a very good New Year
Justin Thadd Kludzinski

Jaimie

You hang with the papa (Doc) vampire
With Sif you get to were armor
I think you really like Thor
The stand is almost your last
They built you as Jessi XX
I think it was a very good job
Lucy is good because she caught you
Body guards watch over me
Some times it no good to find a Rest Stop
I see the dark world coming
You guest on covert affairs
You have a picture in a dress sitting down
Is flying sauce what you found
Play me something on the Guitar
Witchy Women you are
North Carolina is Far
You are in LA as a Star
By: Justin Thadd Kludzinski

Johnny

I seen do the Jump
As Edward you would cut us into a stump
Sam looked out for Benny and Joon
Barnabas could only see the Moon
Gilbert really did like grapes
Jack the pirate fought a sea snake
Frank was so cool on the train
George got bad and was close to insane
Ichabod did lose his head
Donnie could end up dead
Sheldon did just lose an eye
I know Tonto did his thing
Mad was cool but did not sing
John was the public
Sweeney did not sublet
I hope you like this anyway
I see your movies everyday
Justin Thadd Kludzinski

Julia

I was enchanted by Mystic Pizza
You had my heart in Pretty Women
The Pelican Brief was the kind of suspense I like
My best friends wedding
Put your conscience to the test
I am a leukemia survivor
I watch Dying Young
I was told not to watch it
I did find out why
I had thoughts of rebelling
I was going to say heck with it
No more Chemo for me
Runaway Leukemia patient not bride
I then thought of God and family of mine
The Sleepy with the Enemy was also great
I glad you one the Oscar for Erin a true story
You were a dialysis patient in Steel
I fix dialysis machines
My friend's daughter had a Kidney transplant
I had a bone marrow transplant in 2/12/2012
I hope AML is behind me
So I guess I will leave you
You are a great actress
So send us all some new gems
May you someday do one my books
I writing number two
I have 25 more two write
I sure one will fit right
I say good bye for now so sleep tight
Justin Thadd Kludzinski

Michelle (Mimie)

I think you are so beautiful
I know that others do too
I seen a different side of you
I see that you show us kittens
I have seen your cartoons too
I have love your Paris pictures
I like your languages to
I believe you speak Polish also
I know you know French
I communicated in English hope you do not mind
I like your sexy pictures you always show us class
I like pictures of red rose
I think you love art portraits
I think you are a deep thinker
I know you hide it well
I know your friends do love you
I guess it is mostly men some how
I do think you are good to women
I seen a child's picture I think you love them too
I have talk to much about you
So I now bid you au revoir
By: Justin Thadd Kludzinski

Rihanna

The sun is out were you were born
The pirates landed on your shores
The dance of yours of in "what's my name"
The time you sang "Only Girl (in the world)"
The American Music Awards we found love
The ocean is something you know one in east and one in west
Which one do you love best
The trick of umbrella it not just for rain it is for the sun
The sun can be hot very much like you
The parish I went was just like yours it was Saint Michaels
The arch angel watches and knows what we do
The other is disturia that quite for sure
The one that promise diamonds is the one that cast down
The boy that is rude he works for this guy
The pictures of Eve as she lay on ground
The boy name Adam was no were around
The one that did tempt her was never found
The eyes must be open for he still in town
The wings of our angels protects us from harm
The story is going and we can find love
The Lord brings us comfort from way above
The hour is pass I must be off
Till next time my friend I see you again
By: Justin Thadd Kludzinski

Sly

The dog you had was a mastiff
You had couple of turtles call cuff and link
Rambo had Vietnam veterans happy
They know that one day America will accept them
Their parade and honor not found
When he went full circle and got back to his father's farm
Rocky is everyone's love story of a man you always root for
His wife is a gem that he discovered
Sometimes he went over the top
He even found paradise alleys
Fought a alien on a cliff
Work hard and fast as Nighthawk
The coolest car in Cobra
Assemble a band of Expendables
A judge that must always be right
Escape if you help build the prison
You Put a Bullet in the Head
Wesley needed some Demolition
Your write very good stories your our new John Wayne
By: Justin Thadd Kludzinski

Sylviane

Your eyes are blue as can be
Your hair very blonde as I hope it would be
Your style always the best
Your European nature that is all very great
Your family means much to you now
Your Friends like Manfred know how
Your always on time or is my mistake
Your color is pink by the way
Your train stops here and there
Your never alone you have many friends
You're signing Karaoke as I write right now
Your friend has a beautiful car
Your car must be red
Your couch it is blue
Your kitchen is green
Your boyfriend is jealous too
Your weakness is chocolate I think
You're a new friend and I bid you adieu
By: Justin Thadd Kludzinski

Manfred

I know you like Grand Prix
You know beautiful women
The horses are things you like
A right for a baby is yours all the same
You can not see one murdered
As a father myself I would never think it
You know many singers
You have show me them all
You work with a hard hat but use your mind
You have the best beer of all the time
Your white wine is special
There is no doubt of that
So Prost to you my friend
May I return to Germany one day again
So when you go on your next Folk Marsch or Oktoberfest
Have a liter of Spaten and look to the west
By: Justin Thadd Kludzinski

Dreams

I wake in silent of the morning
I wonder of the dream I just had
I see the sun's glimmer approaching
I think of my love in my dream
I here the birds as sing here
I kiss and embrace her forever
I look to bed were she would lay
I brush her hair from her neck as I do kiss her right there
I see her cat name named Pixy looks for her now
I then make love to her gently
I call her but there is no answer
I talk to her low and real quiet as not to wake the children all sleeping
I know that I have really lost her
I listen as she plans our future
I think she is watching me as an angel
I kiss and tell her goodnight
I hope to see her tonight
By: Justin Thadd Kludzinski

Dragon Heart

I know a dragon is in me
He seldom comes out
His tongue is wild and long
The night is all about sounds
Kisses are meant to last long
She must meet my lips slowly
Eyes gaze with dreams and soft longing
Her breast I suckle the right one first
Third base is were I spend time
It like a very fine wine
Now it time to move on
The fire is about to engage
A morning of true romances
It has become many and long
Dragon heart has taken chances
But love is a part of this song
Justin Thadd Kludzinski

Hello Cowgirl in the Sand

I lay you down on desert sand
You skin so bronze
The scorpions dare not come around
Snakes craw the other way
We make love all night and day
Coldness of dessert
Is challenged by our burning hearts
Your hat is gone to burning winds
Your red kerchief is all that remains
You give me a cry of joy
I bring you closer like a toy
Would we know this passion again
Or is a cowgirl's sin
Am I a bandit of your dreams
Or the good sheriff in your life
It is for you to dwell on here tonight
Justin Thadd Kludzinski

Serenade

I like the story of serenade
Maria did tell me one day
She was in Honduras for a year
Some one else next door had a suitor
He sang and brought his three musician friends
Maria and Solitaire her cousin peered though the drapes
It was a beautiful thing the girl's mom came first
Then she let her daughter enjoy
She told him yes and the rest is history I guess
I wish I could be as clever as them
I do like romance it makes you alive
The things that you do that make you as one
The kiss and stuff we leave it right there
It is words that you say and action you show
Parking and talking till its too late
The looks of her mother when finally get her home
I like the dare and the love we did share
She had own tape it was call love a cat
We even went to see Fleetwood Mac
Kenny Loggings was to opening act on Rumors tour
I bought her a red t shirt and floppy red hat
I whisper sometimes Maria come back
The landslide always brings me down
By: Justin Thadd Kludzinski

153

Rendezvous

It happens between a man and a woman
Is it right or wrong
Are they married or single
Do they love or is it lust
A small hotel room late at night
Making love through out the night
She screams her passion
He falls exhausted his life force gone
They snuggle silently and embrace
Who make the move to leave first
The best is if no one till maid comes in
That means more love making
It can be great
Let the consequences wait
Someday it might be your love story to tell
Forget other people hearts tell the truth
Can you but think of passion inside
Waiting for a return of love on the side
Justin Thadd Kludzinski

Mysterious Woman

Some times a woman is a shadow
She is hard to see at all
Kisses do not faze her
Giving her attention
Is like a wine with concord grapes
All she wants is more
Your sweat is barley noticed
Till her passion gives her reason to call
A cigarette and cup of coffee
With out a hair out place
With her make up on great
Just a kiss for goodbye
She is flying out of the door
I wonder why
Am I a rendezvous
Or something special to you
Love is in my heart
Is passion only in yours
My mysterious woman of the night
Justin Thadd Kludzinski